THIS IS NOT A SUTRA:
A Trial and Error Guide
to Meditation for Secular Thinkers

THIS IS NOT A SUTRA

A Trial and Error Guide to Meditation for Secular Thinkers

CHAD FRISK

COPYRIGHT © 2016 CHAD FRISK
ALL RIGHTS RESERVED

THIS IS NOT A SUTRA:
A TRIAL AND ERROR GUIDE TO MEDITATION FOR SECULAR THINKERS

This book is dedicated to anyone who wants to take a closer look at their life without committing to a particular belief system.

Acknowledgments

This book would not exist without the help of a number of different people. I'd like to acknowledge as many of them as I can:

Thanks to Tucker Peck for providing incisive commentary on an early draft.

Thanks to editor Wes Matlock for his professional treatment of the final manuscripts. This book would have been much less coherent without him.

Thanks to Dana Johnson for his incredible design work, both on the interior of the book, the cover, and the ebook. His professionalism and style never fail to impress me.

Thanks to Shigemi Matsushima for taking me to a Zen temple to be tortured all those years ago.

Thanks to Luke Marshall for his comments on a different book that eventually became this one.

Thanks to Mike Rathwell for telling me that that first book wasn't very good.

Contents

FOREWORD — xi

INTRODUCTION:
Entering the Maze — 1

PRACTICE #1:
Focus — 17

PRACTICE #2:
Insight — 37

PRACTICE #3:
Positive Emotion Boosters — 57

PRACTICE #4:
Visualizations — 85

FINAL THOUGHTS:
Walking the Maze — 93

APPENDIX:
Further Reading — 97

Foreword

In the book you're about to read, Chad says: "I don't claim to be anyone special. What I am is a regular person who spent years beating himself over the head with spiritual texts because he thought there might be something of value in them. Doing so gave me a headache, but it also knocked out a few jewels."

I think this is a wonderful description of what makes this book so worth reading. Chad's work is unique in that it's the story of a regular guy learning to meditate. While many meditation books claim to be written by "regular" people, those regular people seem to have hundreds of devotees and bestselling books, making it fairly difficult to really believe that if they can do it, you can too. If you're a beginning meditator, they're just not very similar to you.

For better or worse—actually, for both better and worse—Chad really typifies the types of students I've seen drawn to meditation. He's intelligent, curious, and interested in improving his mental and emotional wellbeing. He also has the all-too-common tendencies to beat up on himself for feeling like he's not doing well enough when he's actually doing great, and the tenacity to stick with something he should really have given up on because it doesn't work. Perhaps this sounds familiar.

If you're looking for books and articles on why you should want to meditate, you will not find the slightest shortage. However, if you're looking for books on how to actually do it, you may find yourself limited to a pretty small number of sources. The vast majority of those manuals give you instructions. Do this. Don't do that. Rinse, and repeat.

The most common thing new meditators tell me is something along the lines of "I am bad at meditation. Unlike all of the other people who are naturally able to quiet their minds, I have the unique and quirky attribute that my unique and quirky mind just keeps racing and thinking all the time. I've concluded, therefore, that meditation is for other people, not for me." So, if your meditation manual is simply telling you what to do, you might get frustrated. And if the person who says "I did it, so you can too" just sold 3,000 tickets at $100 each for a talk they're giving on spirituality for their international bestseller, you may find their argument pretty unconvincing.

I met Chad because, technically, he is my meditation student. I say "technically" because he is nearly-always absent from my class. If he died, it might be months before I found out. As you'll read in the book, this is one of many examples of Chad not being what some might consider the ideal meditator. If he has any unusual spiritual or psychological talents above-and-beyond the average person, he believes that he has yet to find them. His great talent, however, is his ability to communicate. In one of the most relatable and understandable books on meditation I've ever seen, Chad describes the pros and cons of various meditation techniques, as well as how he came to have so much information on the subject. By reading this book, you'll get to know Chad well enough that when he says "I did it, so you can too," you might be convinced that he's telling the truth.

Beyond simply the story of a regular person developing the meditation practice they wanted, Chad's book provides an incredibly accurate and detailed description of various types of meditation practices, as well as instructions for how to do them. While you will assuredly enjoy his style and personal stories, he provides an uncommon wealth of information about meditation. There are not many books you might read and then feel able to start a meditation practice, but I think this is one of them.

For anyone who wants to learn to meditate, fears they might not be much good at it, and is certain they won't be much good at adhering to invariant step-by-step instructions, this book is a gem. I hope you enjoy it as much as I did.

Tucker Peck, PhD
Tucson, Arizona

INTRODUCTION:
Entering the Maze

I STOOD IN THE SPIRITUALITY SECTION of the bookstore, nursing a splitting headache.

I wanted to meditate, but none of the books made any sense. I leafed through Hindu, Taoist, Buddhist, and (alas) New Age texts, trying to interpret the seemingly uninterpretable.

I failed.

I originally got interested in meditation through brain science. The work of researchers like Richard Davidson, psychiatrists like Daniel Siegel, and journalists like Daniel Goleman suggested that meditation could have dramatic cognitive benefits for those who practiced it. The promises of clearer thinking, greater resilience, and improved interpersonal relationships were appealing to me.

Unfortunately, their work didn't make it clear exactly *how* to meditate. To learn that, I had to find meditation instructions. Quickly, I discovered a whole genre dedicated to providing them: the meditation manual.

I was excited, but my excitement soon waned; many of the meditation manuals I encountered came from traditions I was unfamiliar with, and their instructions didn't make a lot of sense to me. To make things worse, I didn't know anyone who meditated, so my only choice was to figure it out on my own. It was sink or swim, and—unfortunately—I sank all the way to the bottom. I stopped laughing. I largely stopped speaking. I tried to stop thinking. I did all of the things I thought the texts were telling me to do, and I started to lose my mind.

But the academic research was relatively clear, the appeal of improved mental functioning was strong, and I was too stubborn to give up. I held on, and eventually I *did* start to figure it out. It turns out that I was doing everything wrong.

Meditation—which, as we will see, is a word that subsumes a number of different practices—is the single most useful mental-training tool that I've found. Through consistent meditation, I have greatly improved a number of valuable life skills, including:

- **impulse-control**
- **rate of occurrence and persistence of positive emotions**
- **empathy**
- **resilience**
- **focus**
- **self-awareness**

I am less reactive, feel less guilt, am less manipulated by negative emotions, and spend less and less time lost in thought (though I'm still lost a fair amount). Before I started meditating, I didn't even realize that these things were problems for me. Maybe you haven't, either.

In this book, I hope to give you the tools to observe your mental life more closely. You may find that it is less healthy than you realized (or you may not, it's impossible for me to say). If you do find that your internal state of affairs is less organized than you would like, there are things you can do about it. In this book, I will introduce you to tools that have helped me begin to sort my mental clutter.

I'm not a master of anything. I'm not a superhero. I have bad days and I get in funks, but I get in less of them than I used to, and they don't last nearly as long. Meditation is the reason why. I went through something like hell to get here; I wrote this book so that you don't have to.

Well, let me take that back. I wrote this book so that you won't have to stay there as long as I did.

Why Read This Guide?

The fact that you're reading this book suggests that you have some interest in exploring a meditative practice, which I think is great. But where should you start? The shelves of bookstores are packed with meditation manuals, and it's difficult to know which to read.

I have read a lot of them, and—if you remain interested in meditation after reading this book—you might want to as well. It's important to look at the practice from a variety of perspectives. If you don't, you risk falling into the trap of believing that any single perspective illuminates the one true way. I've been there, and that belief locked me into a sense of rigidity that made honest, open inquiry—what I have come to believe is the best use for meditative practices—quite difficult.

So what does this guide add to the conversation? Why read it as opposed to any other?

I can think of two reasons. The first is that many of the meditation manuals on the market come from traditions that are unfamiliar to many people born and raised in Western countries.[1] As a white male born and raised in Seattle, Washington, I found some of the more metaphysical beliefs occasionally expressed in versions of Tibetan Buddhism, for example, to be very perplexing. At times, this made some of their meditation instructions hard to carry out.

---

1 It is my understanding that the division between "Western" and "Eastern" countries is deeply problematic, to say nothing about the complex relationship between countries, cultures, and ways of thinking. There is a vast body of literature dedicated to unpacking and critiquing these divisions. I use the term 'Western' here as an expedient to refer to countries in which many dominant cultural paradigms trace their lineage through Europe.

THIS IS NOT A SUTRA

There are, of course, plenty of meditation manuals written by Westerners, who know where readers like me are coming from. Even so, the authors of these manuals do sometimes make faith claims that may be hard for outsiders to accept. I personally have never been a monk and try to cleave to a scientific view of the way the universe works (to the extent that I understand it), and some texts were hard for me to utilize because I couldn't accept the worldviews in which their instructions were embedded. In this book, I attempt to present a few meditative practices in terms of my own cultural beliefs, which are (more or less) based upon the methodologies and assumptions of what might be called Western science.

The other reason to read this book is that it's full of mistakes. Not proofreading mistakes, hopefully, but mistakes I made as a meditator. Most books do a good job of explaining what to do, but they don't go into as much detail about what can go wrong when you try.

Each of the four sections of this book is divided into three parts. The first part of each section is a **description of a practice**, along with reasonably simple and specific instructions on how to perform it. The instructions represent a synthesis of what I've read in a number of different books.[2]

The second part of each section is a detailed story of **how I tried and failed** at each practice. While the meditation instructions are simple, I ran into a lot of problems when I tried to perform them. By making my struggles clear, I hope that you will feel comfortable acknowledging and engaging with your own as they come up.

The third part of each section is an attempt to explain **what I have learned** from those struggles. For the most part, I have found a path through the confusion of my early attempts at meditation. Some of what once seemed irrational about the practices now makes sense. Some of what seemed to make sense now strikes me as probably wrong. You are by no means obligated to reach the same conclusions

---

[2] What I consider to be the most useful of these are included in an appendix at the end of this book.

that I have.[3] But I hope that presenting them will at least give you something to investigate.

I don't claim to be anyone special. What I am is a regular person who spent years beating himself over the head with spiritual texts because he thought there might be something of value in them. Doing so gave me a headache, but it also knocked out a few jewels.

In this book, I will do my best to present those jewels in a way that I hope will be accessible to an audience that shares my background. Some of the things I say will be strange. I hope you will treat them as a series of hypotheses to be tested. I will tell you how to do so. The challenge then is to follow the evidence wherever it leads.

What to Expect

This is not a long book, because meditation is for doing, not talking about. In order to do it, however, you need some pointers. Of the very large number of meditative practices that people engage in, I will explain the ones that I do, how I had trouble with them at first, and the corrections I've made over time.

Then you will do them, or you will not. I wish there was a different way to put it, but that's what this boils down to.

Here is a list of the practices I will explain:

- **Focus Practices**
- **Insight Practices**
- **Positive Emotion Boosting Practices**
- **Visualization Practices**

Focus Practices are pretty self-explanatory. They will help you focus on what you want to for longer periods of time.

---

[3] It's worth noting that I will inevitably change my mind about some of the things I say in this book. Nothing here is final, but rather represents my understanding as of this writing.

THIS IS NOT A SUTRA

Insight Practices help you investigate the actual qualities of your everyday experience. You will take a closer look at your **bodily sensations**, your **feelings**, your **thoughts**, and the **relationships between things in the world**. If you're like me, you'll be surprised to find that close application of attention changes the way you experience these phenomena, often in ways that lead to less anxiety and more wellbeing. Be prepared, however: you will probably have to challenge some of your beliefs, which can be unsettling. I'll talk about how I have dealt with this so that you'll be more ready for what comes than I was.

Positive Emotion Practices train the states of mind that allow you to approach challenges with a constructive attitude. Many of life's difficulties reduce to dealing with destructive emotions. These practices will help you access useful mental states more easily. These states include **goodwill**, **compassion**, **poise**, and a state that some call **positive empathy**. I will explain exactly what I mean by these terms when we get to this section.

Visualization Practices are a way to take advantage of the link between mind and body. We will explore a few **classical**[4] **mental images** (along with a couple of **my own creation**) in an attempt to discern whether they have a consistent effect on your physiology. I think they do—and the effects are worth wanting.

Like any other training program, meditation takes effort. You have to get to the meditation cushion, and you have to sweat. Life is full of things to do, and taking twenty minutes to sit in your room rarely seems like a priority. Starting a consistent practice is the first challenge.

The challenges are about more than just investment, however. Many of the practices involve looking at the world in a very different way. This can be disorienting. Things will probably go blurry before they come back into focus.

But they will come back into focus, and the clarity is worth the effort—and the confusion. At least, it has been for me. Maybe you'll find that the same is true for you.

Let's start with the absolute basics.

---

4 In Buddhist contemplative traditions.

Things You'll Want

Meditation is not an expensive hobby. You don't need very much, but you do need a few things. The following is a short list of those things.

A Room

You will want a **room**. It doesn't necessarily need to be the same room every day, though some believe that designating a meditation spot helps establish a regular schedule.[5] At the very least, you will want a space where you can spend some quiet time without being interrupted.

    I meditate in my bedroom. It's not the best place. I'd prefer to meditate in a massive hall or on an isolated promontory overlooking mountain peaks, but it takes a lot of work to get to those places. My room is good enough.

A Commitment

Starting a meditation practice is tricky. You won't want to meditate unless you can see the benefits, but you won't see any benefits until you have practiced for a while. There is no choice but to **commit** to trying in the face of uncertain results. The only way that I have personally been able to maintain a regular practice is to write it into my schedule. I'd recommend doing the same. Meditate once a day at a given time for a week and then decide whether or not you'd like to continue.[6]

---

5 I agree.
6 I think that a meditative practice is best conceived of as a habit. When I allow myself the choice of whether to meditate or not, I choose "not" more often than I would like. Habits, however, are automatic. When meditation becomes a habit, you do it without thinking. This, I think, is the only way to sustain a practice over the long term. I highly recommend Charles Duhigg's book *The Power of Habit* for more on the behavioral ramifications of habits and how to replace undesirable ones with those of your choosing.

A Body, and Postures to Put It In

It doesn't matter what shape your body is in. Wherever you are right now is a perfect place to start.

The first step in meditation is to take your perfectly suitable body and put it in a particular position. There are four primary ones: **sitting**, **lying down**, **standing**, and **walking**. I don't use all of them, but I will briefly introduce each, starting with the ones I use least frequently.

Standing

You can meditate **standing up.** In some traditions, I have heard that the standing position is utilized when you're too sleepy to sit. It is, apparently, an effective way to keep from dozing off.

I don't personally stand during my designated sessions. Rather, I think of the standing pose as a way to steal moments of meditation during the day. I spend a lot of time standing around: I stand in line; I stand in elevators; I stand on street corners, waiting for lights to change. You can meditate while doing all of those things. Precisely how will become clear as we delve into the actual practices.

Walking

Of all the meditation postures, **walking** is the most likely to make you feel like a doofus, because you will probably be seen, and you will probably look silly.

Have you ever seen an elderly or young person doing Tai Chi in the park? Perhaps in the morning? In colorful spandex? Kudos to those people. It takes a lot of courage to exercise in public when you know people are probably laughing at you.

From the outside, walking meditation can look as silly as Tai Chi. Walking meditation entails walking very slowly—and nothing else. You walk, paying careful attention to the way each step feels. The truth is that taking a step feels like a lot more than we usually notice. There's the feeling of the soles of your shoes against the ground, of your feet sliding around inside of your shoes, of the flex and release of the muscles in your calves, quads, hips, abs, butt, etc. Every step is an instance of masterful cooperation between diverse networks of muscle and bone.[7] Walking meditation is about appreciating that complexity.

Some meditation teachers speak very highly of walking meditation. Culadasa, "the director of Dharma Treasure Buddhist Sangha in Tucson, Arizona and author of *The Mind Illuminated: A Complete Meditation Guide Using Buddhist Wisdom and Brain Science*"[8] (which is, incidentally, my number one recommendation for meditation manuals), recommends walking meditation as a necessary complement to seated meditation. While walking, he recommends breaking each step into three parts: **raising the foot** off the ground; **moving it forward** in space; and then **lowering it** back to the ground. The goal is to be aware of the sensations in one foot and leg as they move through these three segments. You can try walking incredibly slowly with your arms still at your side, or you can try to follow the sensations as you walk normally.

Lying Down

This one is nice sometimes. You just lie down and do any of the things we will talk about. It is particularly recommended for use with the **Body Scan**, a practice we will encounter in the Focus section. The only danger with this posture is that you might fall asleep. At that point you will no longer be meditating, but at least you will be taking a nap.

Sitting

This is the position everybody thinks of when they hear the word meditation—and for good reason: it is the primary posture. I'll describe the basics and leave the calibration to you.

Sitting on the ground is an effective position (if you can manage it). It's effective because it is stable (you won't move around too much) without being too effortless. The lying-down position is very stable,

---

7 And other things that the doctors and nurses out there can speak to.
8 As he represents himself on his website, http://culadasa.com/.

THIS IS NOT A SUTRA

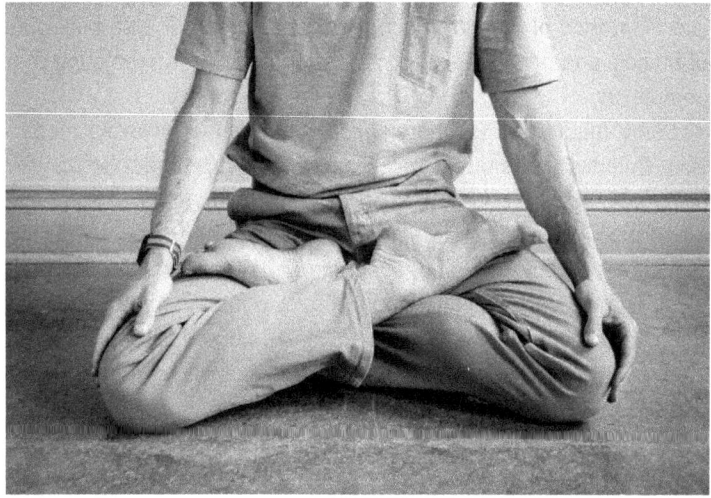

Fig. 1. Full Lotus Pose

but people tend to fall asleep when using it (at least I do). Sitting on the ground requires a little bit of effort to maintain your posture. That effort may help you stay awake.

At first, sitting on the ground was incredibly painful for me because my legs were made of something that didn't bend. After five intermittent years of pain, now they bend well enough. Yours will too, in time. If you want to sit on the ground, here are some things to consider.

You'll probably want a **cushion** of some sort. I bought a meditation cushion online, and I really like it, but you don't need to buy one. You can use a rolled-up towel or a blanket. The key is to raise your butt off the floor to the point where it's easy to sit with your back straight. Experiment with different heights until you find one that works.

You'll probably want to work on your **posture**. When I started meditating, my posture was horrible: my shoulders were slouched, my back was bent, and my legs were bunched up like a sloppy bow on a birthday present.

You can sit with a slouch. It's ok; you won't die. But you might not be able to breathe very smoothly, and after a few minutes your back might start to hurt. The practice of meditation is in part about main-

Fig. 2. Half Lotus Pose

taining focus on an object of your choice (more on that later). Poor posture will probably lead to physical irritation, which then typically leads to mental irritation. Gradually correcting your posture will help reduce the amount of distractors that scatter your attention—and believe me, there will be plenty of them.

The meditation literature recommends stacking the bones of your spine like gold coins. See if you can figure out how to do that. I find that the key to my posture is my lower back. Everything pivots around it. Maybe your body works the same way.

You might want to cross your legs. The point is to make your sitting position as stable as possible. It's hard to maintain focus if you constantly have to shift your body around. You can stabilize your sitting position in a number of ways. What is known as the **full lotus** is supposedly very stable (Fig. 1). I can't do it for more than five seconds so I don't know.

The **half-lotus** is also quite stable (Fig. 2). That's what I do. You can modify it by lowering both legs to the ground (Fig. 3). I like that position too.

When I started out, I was concerned about finding the perfect pos-

Fig. 3. Sitting Pose

ture. This was an unhelpful attitude, because I don't think there's a way to measure perfect. A good posture is one that provides a **stable base** while still being **reasonably comfortable**. Try different things until you find something that works for you.

If you can't cross your legs at all, then you might want to **use a chair**. The key to using a chair is to sit with your back straight and your chest out. Think of how an army cadet sits in a chair. Try that.

Try slouching. See how that feels. Does it affect the way breath flows through your body? If you find that your breathing is strained and uncomfortable, try a different position.

Try a comfortable chair. Try an uncomfortable chair. I don't know what's going to work for you. You are the only person who can figure that out. I've heard that some people recommend putting a pillow on the chair. Getting your hips higher than your knees—which results in a pelvis that slants downward[9]—may make you more alert. Try a bunch of stuff. Keep what works.

Whether seated on a chair or the ground, you'll want to keep your

---

9 Thanks to Tucker Peck for this tip.

Fig. 4. Hands Cupped in Lap

hands in the same place throughout your session. The most commonly taught hand position is to place the right hand on top of the left with the two thumbs touching (Fig. 4). You can also rest a hand on **each knee** if you like. The main thing is to keep them from constantly moving. Set them somewhere, and then leave them there.

Different traditions say different things about what to do with your **eyes**. Some recommend keeping them **half-open**, while others recommend that they be **closed**. I personally meditate with my eyes closed to keep myself from being distracted by external sights. That helps me focus more exclusively on internal sensations.

A Timer

Once you've figured out what to do with your body, you'll want a **timer** for your sessions. In the past, I have used a phone app called **Insight Timer,** which is free. Other people recommend an app called **Headspace**. Headspace has both a **timer** and **guided meditations**, and comes highly recommended by Tim Ferriss. The interface is both aesthetically pleasing and very user-friendly. As of this writing, I've been experimenting with it for only a few days, but I've seen enough to echo

THIS IS NOT A SUTRA

Tim Ferriss's recommendation. I think it is a wonderful tool for beginning (and experienced) meditators. I've written a more complete review in the appendix. One thing to mention about Headspace is that, while free to download, most of the features require a paid monthly subscription.[10] You can try a series of ten guided meditations before choosing whether or not to purchase the subscription.

Whichever timer you end up using, the trick is to set it and forget it. This is surprisingly difficult. I find myself frequently fighting the impulse to check the time. "Maybe it didn't start!" I tell myself, even though I watched it start. "Maybe it broke!" I worry, even though it hasn't been acting up. "Maybe the volume is off!" I reason, even though I heard the opening bell.

The reasons to check the timer are endless. Sometimes I successfully ignore them; sometimes I fail. One time, the volume actually was off, and I found I had meditated for an extra five minutes (!).

One big question is how long to set the timer for. If you're anything like me, you might want to start with **5-10 minutes.**[11] See how that goes. If you feel good, extend the time. Quantity is less important than quality.

What exactly is quality in the context of meditation? In general, it is time spent **actively engaged** in whatever practice you happen to be doing. For example, if you're trying to follow the movement of your stomach as you breathe, in a quality moment of meditation you will be either clearly aware of the position of your abdomen, or you will notice that you are distracted (at which point you gently readjust your attention). If you find yourself tallying up the fantasy football points you earned last week, then you are having a low-quality moment of meditation.

When I first started meditating, I set the timer for thirty minutes because I thought I had to. The majority of those thirty minutes were wast-

---

10   That isn't necessarily a bad thing. Sometimes paying for a service functions to strengthen your commitment to using it.

11   Five minutes is a very short meditation time. If it gets you in the door, however, meditating for five minutes is way better than setting a more intense goal you immediately give up on.

ed alternately zoning and stressing out. I wish I'd focused on significantly shorter bursts of more focused concentration until I got the hang of it.

So when do you add more time? For me, it made sense to add time only when I was able to sit for longer periods without feeling overly agitated.[12] When ten minutes became easy, I moved to fifteen. When I was able to stay engaged more or less consistently for the whole fifteen minutes, I moved to twenty. The longest time I've ever sat for is one hour. An hour is difficult for me, however, so I usually go for around thirty minutes. Ideally, I'd like to sit for forty-five. I certainly had to work up to that amount of time. Start where you're comfortable and extend the time as it seems reasonable.

That does it for the nuts and bolts. Let's turn to the practices themselves.

Summary of the Basics

- Experiment with meditating while **walking**, **standing**, **lying down**, or **sitting**. Sitting on a cushion is the most common way of meditating, but it may take a little bit of time until you feel comfortable doing so.
- Get a **timer** or download **Headspace** and start with short, focused sessions. Five to ten minutes is a good starting length. As you get comfortable with sessions of that length, extend the time, perhaps by five-minute increments.
- Find a **room** in which you won't be disturbed. If you live with roommates or family members, you may have to let them know that you'll be meditating and would like some uninterrupted time. It may be uncomfortable to tell them this, but in order to build a practice you will first have to normalize it, at least in your own mind. People will probably think you're weird. That's fine.
- **Designate a time to meditate** and write it on your calendar. This makes it much more likely that you will actually do it.

---

12 Some degree of agitation is unavoidable, especially at the introductory stages of a practice.

PRACTICE #1:
Focus

BEFORE I STARTED TRAINING MY MIND, I didn't realize that it was a mess. I had graduated from college, had a job, and was more or less competent in daily life. I thought that my mind was under control.

That's not to say that my mental life was free of issues. I worried about worst-case scenarios that never materialized. I replayed conversations in my head, rephrasing them so that I came out looking OK. I tried to read other people's minds, and usually didn't like what I thought I found. Like most people (I assume), I was riddled with neuroses. I just didn't think there was anything I could do but live with them.

This feeling persisted until after I graduated from college, when I developed a serious interest in brain science and psychology. I read incessantly. The books challenged my beliefs that mental habits couldn't be changed. They spoke about people who had overcome the same hang-ups I had, and the tool they often used was meditation. Eventually I decided that I had to try it for myself.

The first practices I encountered were designed to **stabilize attention**—which is to say, to improve my ability to focus. "Pay attention to the sensations of your breath," they said. "Ok," I said and tried to.

It was impossible. I drifted lazily from one thought to the next. I chased other thoughts around with a stick. I got caught up in future fantasies and old memories. Most of the time, my breath was the furthest thing from my mind. Thoughts kept interrupting, and I soon forgot what I was even doing.

Maybe you're more capable than I am. Take the next minute to test your current ability to pay attention. Try to focus on your breath. Feel it as it enters your nostrils, fills your belly, and then flows back out. Don't worry about taking deep breaths. The point of this exercise isn't to make yourself breathe in a particular way, but rather to train yourself to **focus on an object of your choice**. This test determines your baseline. Do it for one minute. You can set a timer if you like.

How did it go? Were you able to keep your attention on the sensations produced by the breath, or did you start thinking about other things? If your attention wanders like mine, then maybe you did a lot of thinking and not a lot of observing.

The mind wanders. That's what it does, at least in my experience. It seems reasonable to suggest that this is a consequence of our evolutionary history. While the relationship between **mind** (by which I mean the contents of subjective experience[1]) and **brain** (the physical organ between our ears) isn't entirely understood,[2] we do know that brains are constantly scanning the environment for threats.

This is good. Our brains developed in dangerous territory. It was important for our ancestors to be hyper-alert, because taking it easy was a good way to get eaten. Even though most of us (at least, perhaps, those reading this book) no longer live in similarly dangerous environments, our brains are still calibrated for them. In other words, our brains are biased to find threats, regardless of how likely those

---

1 This is by no means a comprehensive definition of mind. Few even agree upon what mind is, which makes defining it rather difficult. For the purposes of this book, thinking of the mind as the contents of subjective awareness will help us get started with the practices. If you read more in this field, you will come across more in-depth analysis of this topic (some of which is probably on-point).

2 Exactly how much we (think we) understand varies widely depending upon who you ask.

threats are to cause actual harm. If this process gets out of hand, it can lead to a chronically engaged stress response, which I find quite unpleasant.

Focus Practices are good for helping you chill out. The more you do them, the less you will feel like a frightened monkey on amphetamines. It will be easier to settle your mind on the stimuli you want, without being distracted by threats that aren't likely to do you any harm.

Hyperactivity isn't the only impediment to concentration, of course. Sometimes you feel dull and disinterested in everything. Other times, your mind locks onto something and won't let go. Focus Practices take on those states of mind as well.

The Practice

The practice is simple. Here are the steps:

❶ **Settle into your position of choice (standing, walking, lying down, or sitting).**
❷ **Select an object of focus.**
❸ **Focus on it.**
❹ **Get distracted.**
❺ **Notice your distraction.**
❻ **Gently return to the object of focus.**
❼ **Repeat steps 4-6.**

That's literally it. It's infinitely simple, but that doesn't make it easy. Let's look at some potential objects of focus.

Your Body

Your body is constantly producing signals, and you can be better or worse at reading them. If you can do so well, we say you have good **body awareness**. Some people have great body awareness—gymnasts, for example. If you tried to use the parallel bars without it, you might kill yourself. I used to have pretty poor body awareness. Luckily, I have been able to refine it with a few techniques.

The Body Scan

The classic technique for developing body awareness is called the **Body Scan**, which I mentioned in the section on meditating while lying down. The Body Scan involves exactly what it sounds like: systematically attending[3] to the sensations produced in different parts of the body.

When doing a body scan, I like to imagine my attention as a red laser. I start by focusing it at the crown of my head (which more often than not feels like a knot of wires). Paying attention to the knot loosens it, which is surprisingly pleasant. I move the laser down, scanning my ears, moving across my face, mapping my forehead, my eyes, my cheeks, my lips, and my jaw, becoming aware of tension and loosening it as I go. I continue the scan, moving into my arms, pooling in the joints of my elbows, slipping into and across each of my fingers. Can you feel your fingertips? Can you feel your fingernails? I can, at least a little bit. Keep going. Torso, hips, quads, kneecaps, calves, ankles. Continue into your feet and down into your toes.

You can perform a Body Scan anywhere and at any time: standing in line at the grocery store, sitting on the bus, talking on the phone, sitting in meetings, or while lying down in your room. The more you do it, the easier it becomes. You may be surprised to notice that your body is tense most of the time. Regularly scanning it will allow you to detect that tension. You can then learn to let go of it.

The Field of Sensation

While the body scan teaches you to be aware of specific body parts, you can also learn to focus on more **general body sensations**. Con-

---

3   Meditation texts often refer to introspection as "attending to" sensation, which may be an unfamiliar usage of the term for many. It is intended to approximate the open, curious, and responsive sort of attention that will ultimately allow you to cultivate a more flexible mental life.

templative types talk about experiencing their bodies as a field of sensation. At first I had no idea what they were talking about. Now, I realize that they're talking about pure phenomenology.

Phenomenology could be defined as the first-person study of subjective experience. What do you *actually* see, hear, smell, taste, or otherwise feel in any given moment? Phenomenology, in the context of this practice, is about handling the threads of bare sensation before they are woven into any sort of story.[4]

It's hard to attend to bare sensation. The impulse to spin sensation into story is incredibly powerful and almost entirely automatic. The stories don't have to be complicated; they can be as simple as a label. But even a simple label covers up the actual experience of things. For example, think of what happens when you drink a cup of coffee. Do you look at the color? Do you notice the smell? Do you parse the taste for hints of cream or sugar?

Or—as is most often true of me—does a light go off in your mind that says "coffee", and then you're done?

The hallmark of sensation is that it slips away, but with practice you can learn to actually feel it before it does. Let your attention rove around the inside of your body, sensing. Zoom in on whatever seems most interesting.

Your Breath

The breath is the most common object of focus. It's good because it's always available. In my initial foray into contemplative circles, I encountered the phrase "follow your breath" a lot, but it took me a long time to figure out how to actually do that. Ultimately, and after a lot of reading, I've settled on two (non-original) techniques: **streaming**, and finding **anchor points**.

Streaming involves following the sensations of a single breath as it moves through your body, whereas anchor points tie your attention to a single, fixed location. Using anchor points is the most com-

---

[4] Mental narratives and their physiological effects do also fall under the purview of phenomenological inquiry, but that's not the object of interest here.

mon way of practicing, and most mediation books advocate it. It is what I currently do. The reason that I include the section on streaming is that it may be an easier way to start out, because streaming allows you to latch onto a wider band of sensations. Once you've developed an ability to focus using streaming, the difficulty involved in focusing on subtler sensations at the anchor points may train your focus more effectively. You can think of streaming like the training wheels to get you started, and anchor points as a vehicle for the longer journey.

Streaming

As I said, streaming is about following the **entire path of a single breath** from start to finish. You follow the front edge of a breath from the point at which it enters your nostrils down through your chest, into the base of your stomach, and then back out. The goal is to feel the sensations that arise in the body as the breath passes through it.

You want to stream the whole breath. The tendency is to get bored halfway through and spiral off into some reverie. In everyday life, we call this daydreaming. The fact is that there is no way to keep yourself from daydreaming (unless you were born with particular skills or have otherwise managed to train them). When you notice that you are daydreaming, congratulate yourself; you can't refocus if you don't first notice that you are distracted.

One trap I fell into was condemning myself when I noticed that I was distracted. I thought that the best way to train myself was with a stick.[5] However, in *The Mind Illuminated,* Culadasa makes the argument that this is counterproductive. By getting irritated, I was teaching my brain that noticing distraction was a bad thing, which—Culadasa argues—makes noticing less likely to happen in the future.

If you train yourself to view the act of noticing distraction as a

---

[5] I use the past tense in this paragraph, but I am still very much in the process of replacing this tendency to self-condemnation with what might be more productive mental habits.

good thing, you will find yourself doing so more frequently. At that point, you can refocus. Slowly but surely, the periods you spend daydreaming will get shorter and shorter.

Anchor Points

Anchor points are what they sound like: places in your body at which you place and maintain your attention. There are two common anchor points: the **stomach**, and the **inside of the nostrils**. Some meditation manuals recommend starting with the stomach and then moving to the nostrils for the same reasons that you might start with streaming and then move to anchor points. The sensations at the stomach are easier to focus on at first, whereas the sensations at the nostrils are subtler (and as such will be both harder to focus on and more fruitful if you can manage to).

When anchoring your attention to your stomach, breathe in through the nose and feel your stomach inflate. Then feel it deflate with the out-breath. (It's common to breathe out through the nose as well.) Think of a channel that connects your nose to the base of your stomach, and imagine your breath traveling through it. If your stomach doesn't move, then you are probably taking shallow breaths with your chest.

Chest breathing wears you out. Before I started meditating, I didn't pay attention to how I was breathing; I didn't even know that there were different ways to breathe. I now know to differentiate between stomach breathing and chest breathing. Once you start paying attention, the difference between the two becomes obvious. Stomach breathing is relaxing, which makes it easier to focus.

Once you find that the you're able to focus on the rise and fall of your stomach, you may consider moving your anchor point to the **opening of your nostrils**. Focusing on sensations there is somewhat more challenging; however, there is a body of research suggesting that a certain degree of difficulty facilitates learning.[6]

---

6 The work of psychologist Mihaly Csikszentmihalyi (pronounced *cheek-sent-mi-high*) on flow states comes immediately to mind, as does research from

If a given task is too easy, it's hard to learn anything from it. At the same time, if it is too hard, you will be unable to focus. Because the sensations at the stomach are easier to detect, they make a good entry-level object of focus. The sensations at the nostrils are harder to detect and might not be useful for you at the beginning of your practice, but later in your practice, that very difficulty makes them a more effective training tool.[7]

These days, I spend the majority of my sessions attempting to focus on the sensations at my nostrils. See if you can feel them. Can you detect the exact moment at which air begins to flow in? Can you detect the exact moment at which the in-breath stops? When you start to pay attention, you'll notice a gap between the in-breath and the out-breath, and another between the out-breath and the following in-breath. You may notice that aiming to be aware of those moments either extends or shortens them. Try to note those differences.

Try also to differentiate between characteristics of the in- and out-breath. Pay attention to differences in air temperature, smoothness, and the exact location within the nostrils at which you feel sensation. You may be surprised by how much is actually going on in there.

So far we've talked about using your breath and your body to stabilize your attention. Next, we'll talk about how to use your mind to do the same. This is likely an unfamiliar concept, so I will do my best to be clear. You may have to experiment with this for yourself to develop a first-person feel for what I'm talking about.

The Space of the Mind

The mind is surprisingly difficult to define. What is it, exactly? Where is it, exactly? It's hard to say, exactly. Earlier, I defined mind as the contents of subjective experience: sights, sounds, tastes, thoughts,

---

cognitive psychology summarized in the book *Make It Stick: The Science of Successful Learning* by Peter Brown, Henry Roediger, and Mark McDaniel.

7 It's worth pointing out that some meditation instructors, notably the Burmese Theravada master U Pandita, feel that the sensations at the stomach provide a sufficient training device even for advanced meditators.

emotions, etc. While that picks out a certain class of mental phenomenon, it leaves out something else: the space in which those objects appear. This is what contemplative traditions refer to as the **space of the mind**. At first I had no intuitive grasp of what that was supposed to be, and so spent a lot of time trying unsuccessfully to define it.

I've come to the understanding that while it's quite difficult to say what the space of the mind *is*, it's not so difficult to *experience*. You can think of the space of the mind as the frame within which thoughts and emotions fit. This frame expands and contracts: sometimes the space is vast and thoughts are tiny pinpricks; other times, the space is so cramped that thoughts fill your entire field of vision.

You can use this space as an anchor for your attention. All you need to do is zoom out. Thoughts will repeatedly zoom in on themselves, but all you have to do is relax and return to a wider focus. Contemplative types have developed a number of metaphors to help do this. I will explore two: **mind as sky**; and **mind as stage**.

Mind as Sky

Imagine that your mind is the sky and that your thoughts are clouds. Different thoughts can be compared to different types of clouds: some are white and fluffy; some are gray; others are black and full of lightning. Attention tends to lock in on the storm clouds, but you don't have to let it stay there. When you find yourself positioned beneath a thought-thunderhead, zoom out. The sky is blue to all sides. If you zoom out far enough, you will see it.

If that doesn't work, you can try a different perspective. Imagine that you're looking at the Earth from the International Space Station. Thunderheads only obscure the smallest part of the planet's surface. The rest glows.

While that sounds kind of hokey, it *is* a reasonably accurate description of the perceptual shift that occurs when you begin to explore and expand this unfamiliar inner space. It may take some trial and error, but you'll figure it out with some effort.

Mind as Stage

You can also experience the mind as a stage. In this metaphor, thoughts are actors who appear on it. The practice involves noting the movement of the actors without losing sight of the stage.

You'll find that some of the actors are noisy. They want to draw attention to themselves. It's not their fault; it's just what they do. But it is kind of annoying. When a thought pulls you in, pretend that you are a director dealing with a prima donna. Don't argue with it. Don't reason with it. Just let it blow off whatever steam it has accumulated. The less you fight it, the quicker it will go to its dressing room.

This particular image draws your attention to the fact that thoughts come and go. Every thought you've ever had appeared at one point and then passed away at another. While it may not be logical to say thoughts come from or go anywhere, they do need a perceptual space to enter and exit. If you soften your attention, you can retain awareness of this space. You'll be more consistently aware that any given thought is just a player in the larger show that is your mental life.

These metaphors might help you, or they might not. I certainly hope they'll be useful, but ultimately they are just tools to assist you in your own private exploration. If you find that they don't make sense, don't worry about it. Quietly pay attention to how your own thoughts work, and you'll develop metaphors of your own.

We've just looked at a basic description of meditation practices for focus. Next, I will describe some of the struggles I had (and still have) with them. You may be able to avoid them. If you aren't, at the very least you'll know that you're not alone.

My Struggles with Focus

While Focus Practices are now an important part of my everyday life, by no means has that always been the case. Establishing a consistent practice was very difficult for two interrelated reasons: **I didn't have a**

clear reason to invest the time and energy; and even when I did actually sit down to practice, **I didn't know what to do**. I'd like to return to the beginning of my practice and explain both my why and how problems. Then I'll share how I continue to work through them. Let's start with the why problems.

Why Problems

For the first few years of my practice, it was never clear why I was doing it. I had read about the supposed benefits, of course. I knew that experienced meditators claimed to be able to sustain focus on chosen objects at length and to be calmer, less reactive, more patient, and generally happier than when they started. But anyone can claim anything, and I didn't have much to go on but their word.

My early forays into the Focus Practices were not reassuring. I sat down and my mind went berserk. I often finished a session feeling less calm, more reactive, less patient, and generally less happy than when I started. "Maybe they were just making it all up?" I started to think.

But there *was* solid research to bolster some of those claims, so I wasn't willing to call bullshit and give up. That said, it was hard to make myself sit down and endure the tornado that was my mind. "I should meditate," I would think. Usually that was as far as I got. Even on those days when I did make it to my improvised cushion, I didn't do it with much enthusiasm. It was hard to imagine that the tornado would ever settle down.

Why Suggestions

After having meditated for five or six years (as of this writing), I have finally seen some of the benefits that the texts talk about. I'm not a master. I can't sit for hours without moving, and my sessions aren't a constant stream of joy. But they are considerably more pleasant than they used to be, and I'm comfortable saying that the benefits spill over into my daily life. What good things may happen if you do the Focus Practices regularly?

First and foremost, you will learn a lot about what distracts you.

Most of us are prisoners in and of our own minds. To paraphrase mediation teacher Joseph Goldstein, every thought is a hook, and we spend most of our lives wriggling on them. Good times are good, but bad times are like being dragged behind a speed boat without skis.

The Focus Practices will make that very clear to you. They have shown me that I have far less control over my thoughts and emotions than I thought I did. The automaticity of my unexamined life was astounding. Before meditating, I was entirely reactive. Thoughts and emotions would emerge in my mind, and the way I responded to them was effectively preordained: I had to chase that worry; I had to fight that fear; I had to engage with that criticism. It was exhausting, but I couldn't do anything about it because I was entirely on autopilot.

Thankfully, the more I looked into my mind, the more obvious my own patterns (both of thought and response) became. I imagine the same will be true for you.

With practice, you may discover that you don't actually have to do anything with your thoughts. You are free to just leave them be. You'll have moments when thoughts can't touch you. You'll sit there, and thoughts will appear as they usually do. But you'll see the hooks, and your attention will stay exactly where you want it to. It is those moments of robust focus that you are aiming for.

Once you can do that on the cushion, you'll find that many of the challenges of everyday life don't affect you as much as they used to. You'll find that things like failure and criticism won't bother you as much. You'll find that traffic no longer upsets you. You'll find that deadlines are less stressful, and that speaking in front of people is less worrisome.

But why? What does focus have to do with any of that?

The main reason this practice has such calming results is that you will learn how to let thoughts dissipate. Thoughts in and of themselves are unproblematic. It is when you fight or fuel them that you get into trouble. The Focus Practices teach you how to be aware of thoughts without fighting them.

Furthermore, you'll train your attention to stay where you'd like. By placing it in a given location and then moving it back when it squirts away (and by doing this over and over again), you are training a skill for future use. Distractions are endless, both while meditating and in daily life, but the more you meditate, the less demanding those distractions will seem.

Ultimately, the only way to get over the "Why meditate?" question is to experience the benefits for yourself. Sadly, you won't see anything resembling a benefit until you've meditated for a period of time. That could be a reasonably short period of time (maybe even as short as a single session if you pay close attention[8]). It took somewhat longer for me because I was impatient. Progress (defined as a more consistent ability to disengage from unwanted distractions) is slow, intermittent, and fleeting; seemingly successful sessions are often followed by miserable ones. I often evaluated the state of my practice based upon the quality of individual sessions, which was a mistake. When things weren't going well, I stopped meditating, sometimes for weeks or months at a time. It's hard to progress when you're not training.

One of the reasons I struggled was that I was impatient, but another reason was that I didn't really understand the practices to begin with. Some instructors say that the only bad meditation session is the one you don't do, and I see a lot of value in that attitude—up to a point. If your meditation session involves pounding your head against a brick wall, I think you would be better off not doing it (though it is possible that pounding your head against a brick wall could be a valuable learning experience). Once I got a more intuitive grasp of what quality meditation feels like, I've been abler to replicate it.

I'd like to help you avoid my mistakes if I can, so in the next section I'll describe how I originally misinterpreted many of the meditation instructions I read. Then I will explain my eventual corrections. You will still have to decode the instructions for yourself, but hopefully I can point out a few dead-ends.

---

8 Such good vibes will probably fade away relatively quickly after meditating, however, at least until you've learned to internalize the practice.

How Problems

I entered meditation with the idea that the point was to achieve greater peace of mind. This isn't wrong. In my experience, greater peace of mind *has been* the (general) result of consistent practice.[9] The actual practice, however, is not about forcing your mind to be at peace. That will not work. The mind could be described as a complex system comprised of many parts that often work at cross-purposes.[10] Mental unrest won't go away because you command it to.[11]

The fundamental misunderstanding that the *results* of meditation were under my conscious control caused me to develop three bad habits that slowed my progress significantly. I attempted to **(a) control my breathing**, **(b) induce relaxation**, and **(c) stop thinking**. I'll say a little bit about each of these so that you'll have an idea of why I believe they impeded my progress. Then, in the next section, I'll explain the corrections I've made.

Manhandling the Breath

Because I believed I could (and was supposed to) make myself calm, I began by trying to control my breath. I forced myself to draw long, slow breaths down into my stomach, hold them there for a number of seconds, and then slowly release them. In a stressful situation, consciously taking a deep breath or two clearly does help you calm down. But the Focus Practices are not about intentionally calming yourself down. They are about developing the capacity for more sustained attention.

---

9 I, at least, have had to travel through considerable internal disturbance along the way. I still experience plenty of it—just less than I used to.

10 See computer scientist Marvin Minsky's books *The Emotion Machine* (which I have read) and *The Society of Mind* (which I have not) for more on this topic.

11 In my experience, mental unrest is the result of unexamined internal tension. Building a more integrated self requires the slow, careful, and often painful work of becoming aware of your contradictory beliefs, and then working to change them (slowly, carefully, and often painfully).

At first, however, I didn't know how to do that. What I did know how to do was force myself to take deep breaths. When that didn't lead to focus, I got frustrated.

JUST RELAX!!!

Many of the mediation manuals I read stressed the important of relaxation. Unfortunately, my primary relaxation strategy was to yell at myself. "You're not relaxing," I thought when I felt myself tensing up. Unsurprisingly, that made me tense up more. "You're supposed to be relaxing!" I then thought, somewhat angrily. My shoulders got even tighter. "God damn it, relax!"

Looking back, I see that my attempts at relaxation were absurd. It's no surprise that when the timer went off, I was usually more stressed out than when I started.

Resenting My Thoughts

"Clear your mind."

People say you should do that, and they're not entirely wrong. The result of a consistent Focus Practice is a clearer mind. But you can't forcibly clear it. You have to let it clear itself.

You may come to experience your thoughts as bubbling up from somewhere, not unlike water from a fountain. When I believed I was supposed to be clearing my mind, my strategy was to struggle with those thoughts.

That was a bad idea.

Think about a running garden hose. Now think about using your thumb to block the flow. It doesn't stay blocked for very long. The pressure builds up and is eventually released in the form of a torrent right in your face. If you were really stubborn (and insanely strong), I suppose you could block the hose until it blew up.

As long as the nozzle is on, water will flow. Thoughts work the same way, but I don't know where the nozzle for thoughts is. I don't think we have access to it, which is probably a good thing. What I do know is that trying to forcibly restrict the flow is a recipe for disaster. You can try it if you want. Feel free to stop when it begins to drive you insane.

How Suggestions

Letting Your Body Breathe

The reason that the breath is such a useful object of focus is that you don't have to do anything to it. Breathing is an automatic process—one that can be influenced by conscious intention, of course, but doesn't need to be. Your body is plenty capable of breathing on its own, allowing you to dedicate your attention to observation.

You can think of the mind as having a certain amount of **mental bandwidth**, or **processing power**. Normally, much of that power is squandered on random thoughts, worries, plans, and fantasies—and without training there isn't much you can do about that.

That's where these practices come in. They are designed to help you attain more conscious control over the movements of your attention. The breath is a very effective support for this purpose. The fact that it can run on its own frees you to observe other things. If half of your conscious attention is engaged giving orders to your breath, then your ability to focus will develop much more slowly than it otherwise would. I had a lot more luck once I let my body breathe on its own and devoted the leftover mental energy to scanning for and correcting the inevitable distractions.[12]

Relaxation as Loosening Tension

My early attempts at relaxation suffered from the same misunderstanding as my early attempts at breathing. While I couldn't force relaxation, eventually I did learn that I could tweak the **upstream factors** that lead to it.

One factor that greatly impacts how relaxed you feel is **muscle tension**. The states of different parts of your body act as signals to

---

12 Earlier, I said that you are better off breathing into your stomach than your chest. This is true. The interesting thing is that your body will do this on its own. You don't need to micromanage it. You set the track along which your breath flows. Then you get out of the way and let it run.

your mind, giving it information on what kind of environment you are currently in. Tense muscles seem to signal that you are in a dangerous environment. Relaxing in a dangerous environment would have been disastrous for our ancestors, so it makes sense that relaxation doesn't arise in the presence of tense muscles.

Luckily, muscle tension is something we can exert control over. After years of trying (unsuccessfully) to induce relaxation directly, I eventually learned to approach it indirectly, through muscle tension. As you use practices like the Body Scan, you will get better and better at tuning in to different parts of your body. You can make it a conscious goal to periodically check in to see how tense your muscles are. Inevitably, they will be tense a lot of the time, so when you find tension, you can practice releasing it. This may be tricky at first. You can think of it like letting air out of a balloon or releasing a clenched fist.

As you practice, you will also become aware of **mental tension**. This is probably caused in part by muscle tension, but has a more demonstrably mental component. You will feel it when your mind is engaged in worry, excessive judgment, evaluation, or generally resisting whatever the current state of affairs happens to be. You can treat this mental tension in much the same way you do physical tension: by unclenching. Once you've learned to recognize mental tension, simply release it in the same way you release muscle tension. With practice you will get the hang of it.

Letting Thoughts Be

Thoughts can be bossy. You're sitting quietly, trying to feel your stomach as it moves up and down. You're not bothering anybody. Your mind is an empty room, and all you want to do is sit in it.

But then a thought barges in and demands that you come with it. This can be upsetting, because you may be under the impression that you have to silence your mind; I certainly was, and I still fall into this trap all of the time. As is probably becoming clear, however, the progressive (but sporadic) quieting of the mind is not something you can cause directly, but rather is the more or less automatic result of considerably more granular, intentional adjustments made with your conscious attention.

Attempting to silence thoughts does not work. It simply makes you agitated, which will in turn cause more thoughts that you think you have to silence. This leads to a downward spiral of self-recrimination that will probably make you hate meditating.

A more helpful way of relating to thoughts is to learn to recognize their presence, and then to let them be. For most of us, thinking is such an automatic process that we don't even realize we are doing it; incessant labeling, explaining, arguing, remembering, and fantasizing are entirely normalized, and we don't know that we can learn to live a different mental life.

The first step to improving your ability to focus is to learn to discriminate between thoughts and your object of focus. Once you've noticed the presence of a thought, congratulate yourself, and then return your attention to what you were focusing on. The crucial thing to realize is that it's not your responsibility to make the thought go away. It is perfectly OK to allow it to remain in the background of your awareness. Without the fuel of your attention, thoughts will eventually fade. As Culadasa says, "Let it come, let it be, let it go." I personally am still working on that, but I think it's a useful approach to thoughts I don't want.

This brings us to the end of the Focus Practices. As your focus begins to stabilize, you may notice that your mind doesn't work the way you always thought it did. The Insight Practices, which we will talk about next, offer some avenues for exploration.

Summary of the Practices

Focusing on the Body

- Try to perform a **Body Scan** while lying on your back. Position the beam of your attention at the crown of your head, and then systematically move it around your body.
- Spend a few minutes attending to the general **field of sensations** produced by your body. If you're having trouble locating the field of sensation, start by focusing in on a particular body part, and then gently relax your attention. Imagine the difference between using a tight and a wide focus lens. The body scan uses a tight focus, the field of sensation a wide one.

Focusing on the Breath

- Try **streaming** the whole breath, tracing its path through your body as if with a laser pointer. You will inevitably lose focus and find yourself lost in thought. That's normal. Your task is simply to recognize that you're lost in thought, and then to shift your attention back to the stream of your breath.
- Try **anchoring** your attention at different points in your body. Let it hover at your stomach. Feel the stomach rise and fall. Wait for the next breath. Center your attention over your nostrils. Feel the in-breath ruffle your nose hair. Feel the out-breath on your upper lip. Experiment with other places to find what works for you.

Focusing on the Mind

- Focus on what contemplative types have called the **space of the mind**. Think of it as the sky in which thoughts float, or the stage upon which thoughts appear, perform, and then leave.

PRACTICE #2:
Insight

AS YOU BUILD UP A CONSISTENT FOCUS PRACTICE, you'll find that your mind becomes less and less scattered. That said, your ability to concentrate will be most pronounced while you are meditating. Daily life presents so many challenges that you may feel like whatever calm you've developed while meditating doesn't translate very well to the world off the cushion; from unreasonable demands at work, to worries about your financial stability, to interpersonal conflicts, there will always be things trying to knock you off balance.

But do you have to let them? Many philosophical and psychoanalytic traditions—from Stoicism to Buddhism to cognitive therapy—suggest that you don't. What really throws us for a loop, they claim, is not the stressors of the world, but rather our own inability to respond effectively to them. Furthermore, our inept responses are a result of basic misunderstandings about how our mental and emotional machinery functions. The potential salve for those misunderstandings, they say, is close observation.

In the Buddhist canon, this type of close observation is known as **Insight Practice**. In my experience, Insight Practices move you from not knowing what's going on to at least having some idea.

Insight Practices involve examining four different components of subjective experience. They are:

1. **Bodily sensations**—the same internal stimuli we examined in the Focus Practices.
2. **Feelings**—specifically our innate and automatic tendency to react to things as pleasant, unpleasant, or neutral.
3. **Thoughts**—including ideas, plans, hopes, dreams, fears, etc.
4. **Relationships**—the ways in which objects in the world are interdependent.[1]

When investigating these four categories of experience, we'll keep in mind three questions. The first is, **"Is this permanent?"** Everything is changing all of the time, but you won't notice if you don't pay attention. I know that I tend to engage with things (situations, people, thoughts, emotions, etc.) as if they will be around forever. They won't, so this attitude has a number of unfortunate consequences. We will explore them later in this section.

The second question is, **"Is this a source of happiness?"** We're all in pursuit of happiness, but unfortunately we don't always know what we're looking for. Some of the things that we think will make us happy end up making us feel bad. Other things that we think will be a pain in the ass turn out to be surprisingly meaningful. At times life seems perverse, but it might just be that we're not paying close enough attention to it. Insight Practices are meant to help you align the pursuit of happiness with the reality of experience. Making good decisions is difficult without good data. The only way to collect data on subjective well-being is to pay attention to what causes it and what does not.

The third question is, **"Is this me?"** This question is a little bit weird at first, but in my experience it has been just as useful as the other two. I used to think I knew a lot about myself, but the truth is that I was wrong

---

[1] I'm taking some liberty with my description of this fourth component. It is often left at "objects in the world," but I chose to call it "relationships" because that is what I want to highlight.

more often than not. I mistook familiarity with my behavior for a deeper understanding of where that behavior came from. Looking closely at the stuff of experience and asking, "Is this me?" may cause you to realize that things you thought were enduring aspects of yourself are merely accidents of history that can actually be discarded (with some work).

Bodily Sensations

If you've been doing the body scan, you're starting to figure out how to tune in to sensations in your body. You've felt the crown of your head, you've felt the soles of your feet, and you've sent the laser of your attention roving through all of spaces between them. Simply paying attention to those sensations constitutes a Focus Practice.

Insight Practices go one step further. While observing, you will ask yourself the three probing questions I mentioned above. These questions will help you dredge up and then challenge your notions about how you experience bodily sensations. The hypothesis is that many of these operating assumptions are wrong. Furthermore, these mistaken beliefs end up causing us unnecessary suffering.

But is that actually true? The only way to know is to experiment for yourself.

1) "Is this permanent?"

It's my experience that bodily sensations are constantly changing. It's also my experience that I am not aware of those changes unless I consciously pay attention to them. The reason this matters is because inattention causes us to focus on our *evaluation* of what we're feeling, rather than on the actual sensations. This can lead us down paths we might not want to travel.

Take two sets of physical sensations: a massage and a stubbed toe. How do we typically experience these two different packets of sensory data? It depends on the person, but unless I really pay close attention, the only things I experience are the simple labels: massage, good; stubbed toe, bad.

Well, so what? What's wrong with ""massage, good," "stubbed toe, bad"?

On one level, not attending to actual sensations is simply a missed training opportunity. If you are interested in living in higher resolution, you have to sharpen your senses through use.

More to the point, when we leave the constantly changing stream of experience and grasp onto passing labels, we grasp at straws. The label "good" is like a hologram that lasts only as long as the massage does. If we fail to remember that those sensations are only temporary, we'll be distraught when the hologram falls apart. The same is true of the pain of the stubbed toe, only in reverse. The pain only lasts for a short time, but pain has a way of filling our entire field of vision. If we ask the pain, "Are you permanent?" we'll more quickly recognize that it is already passing away.

2) "Is this a source of happiness?"

Sometimes our bodies feel good: after a long run, wrapped in a blanket on a rainy day, in other situations that I am too prudish to write about. Of course, our bodies aren't always fountains of pleasure. Sometimes, they feel bad—for example, during a long run, after eating too much cake, or while vomiting into a toilet bowl.

Insight Practices are about giving yourself more accurate information on which to base your decisions. You may notice that you feel bad while pedaling your bike up a hill but great as soon as you get to the top. You may notice that you feel great while spooning chocolate ice cream into your mouth but terrible an hour later. These insights may cause you to change your behavior.

They caused me to change mine. Before I started meditating, I used to think that my body felt good or bad for random reasons. I didn't connect the painful fifteen minutes I spent on the toilet to the three bacon cheeseburgers I had eaten an hour before. Once I started paying attention, however, the links became clear. Now that I know that eating too many bacon cheeseburgers results in intestinal distress for me, I regulate my intake. A part of me is sad about that, but my GI tract is thankful.

3) "Is this me?"

I think it's accurate to say that we identify pretty strongly with our bodies. This is *my* body after all. I'm using *my* hands to type this book, *my* eyes to look at the computer screen, *my* brain to consider its coherency. Thinking this way is normal and sane.

But is it the entire story? The primary enterprise for many meditators is cataloging and deconstructing the feeling we call "the self." What is it? Where is it? Who is it? I think we all have a pretty clear idea of what we *think of* as our self, but the chances are good that we haven't examined that notion very closely.

When you scan the various parts of your body, ask yourself, "Is this me?" Are you your head? Your chest? Your lungs or heart or gut? Are you the blood pumping through your veins? Are you your feet or your toes?

I think few people would claim to be their toes. But how about their face? No part of the human body encodes more personal information than the face, but to what extent are you your face? It seems insane to even ask that question, but I'm not sure I have a good answer. I know that I didn't do anything to get my face. Sure, I might do some work to keep it well-groomed and acne-free (or not, as the case may be), but I don't get any credit for the heavy lifting. My face was drawn up before I was born, specified to a certain degree in genetic recipes that organelles swimming in cytoplasm used to cook it up. I just look in the mirror every morning and think, "Huh. There I am."

I am there. But the question is, what does my face have to do with it? It's not entirely clear, but what I do know is that I have begun to reevaluate what my physical appearance says about me as a person. In some ways, it's far less relevant than I thought it was.

Summary of the Practice

- Either in a formal meditation session or during the course of everyday life, periodically check in with the **sensations of your body**. Observe how sensations **change** from moment to moment. Does attending to the sensations make them change more rapidly or more slowly?

Summary of the Practice (cont.)

- Pay close attention to particularly extreme sensation. What does **pain** actually feel like? Ask "**Is this permanent**?" Try to separate the burning of muscle exertion, for example, from the feeling of wanting it to stop.
- Do the same for **pleasant sensation**, except this time separate the pleasure in your body from your desire for it to stick around (or your fear that it will leave).
- Occasionally ask yourself, "**Is this me**?" Is this headache or this caffeine high "me"? Or is it merely a momentary fluctuation in body chemistry that will soon go away? You may find that depersonalizing uncomfortable sensations makes them easier to endure.

The Good, the Bad, and the Whatever

The second object of insight meditation is your **feelings**.

I get confused by this practice, so I think it's worth taking a minute to explain what the word "feeling" describes here. In the context of this particular practice, a feeling is one of three very specific reactions to any given stimulus: **pleasure, displeasure,** or **neutrality**.

You can think of these feelings like reflexes. When a doctor taps your knee with her rubber hammer, your leg jumps. When you come in contact with sensory stimuli (sights, sounds, scents, tastes, etc.), a feeling arises. It's as if an algorithm coded into the back-end architecture of our minds parses experience and tags it as either good or bad, nice or not-nice, pleasant or unpleasant. Alternatively, some experiences might be tagged as neutral, which is to say as causing no obvious emotional response.

These feelings are not quite emotions as we know them. In the Buddhist phenomenological canon, they are known as *vedana*. Generally, I am hesitant to use words from languages I don't understand, but I introduce this one because I think it is useful for conceptual clarity. To my knowledge, there is no comparable word in English, perhaps because we don't have the same tradition of close internal observation to draw upon.

Those who are interested in talking about this particular phenomenon have a choice. They can either use the word *vedana* as is, make up a new word to fill the conceptual gap in English, or use a word that people are familiar with. Using the Sanskrit word is fine for maniacs like me, but it is probably less palatable for normal people. Furthermore, making up words is a notoriously futile enterprise, which makes the second option unappealing. As such, *vedana* is usually translated as "feeling". This is a source of confusion—for me at least—because *vedana* are not feelings in the same sense that, say, irritation, anticipation, and longing are.

Then what are they? You could call them precursors to feelings. What this means is that *vedana* are sparks that could catch and bloom into full-fledged emotions (like excitement, sadness, or boredom, for example), but won't necessarily do so; they need your attention for a catalyst.

This would all be theoretical nonsense if *vedana* weren't observable. Luckily, they are. The first part of this practice is simply to pay close attention to what happens when sensory data impinges upon your awareness. This can be performed on or off the meditation cushion. *Vedana* can be experienced almost like an echo. You are sitting, trying to meditate, when you hear your roommate making noise in the kitchen. The sound will probably dislodge some *vedana* inside of you. Which ones?

Let's look at an example from off the cushion. You walk past a coffee shop and particles of freshly ground coffee strike your nose hairs. Depending upon your constitution, a certain *vedana* will arise immediately after. You may feel drawn to the coffee. You may feel repelled by it. You may feel nothing. This spark of automatically occurring positive, negative, or neutral affect[2] is what is meant by the word *vedana*. Meditation

---

[2] Affect is a technical term for what could be described as the emotional flavor of a given moment as someone experiences it.

teacher and clinical psychologist Tucker Peck commonly translates *vedana* as **feeling-tone**. I'll use his translation for the rest of this book.

You can go deeper. If the coffee shop happens to be a Starbucks, you may have a different reaction depending on your beliefs about corporations, whether or not you are a stockholder, and your opinions of Howard Shultz. Maybe you smelled the coffee before you realized you were passing a Starbucks. Does a new feeling-tone arise when you look up and see the green and white sign?

Once you've become aware of the existence of feeling-tones, you are ready to observe them more closely. We can pose the same three questions we posed to body sensations.

1) "Is this permanent?"

Can you catch feeling-tones as soon as they arise? If you can, what happens to them? Most of the time, feeling-tones explode like fireworks, filling the space of our minds with different emotions. Some emotions sparkle; others burn things down.

You may find that feeling-tones don't necessarily have to bloom, however. You may find that, if you watch them closely, your feeling-tones start to shoot blanks: they rise and fall like stones lobbed into the sky. Maybe that sounds boring, but maybe it isn't. Maybe some emotions aren't worth living through. The only way to know is to experience the phenomenon for yourself. In my experience, I find that paying attention in this way makes me less likely to blow myself up with emotions like anger and frustration when they are unwarranted or unhelpful.

2) "Is this a source of happiness?"

It might seem obvious that positive feeling-tones lead to happiness, whereas negative and neutral ones lead to unhappiness, but that might not actually be the case. It may be that positive feeling-tones propel you towards activities that cause you misery (think excessive gambling), whereas negative feeling-tones prevent you from doing things that could become great sources of well-being (think about resistance to exercise or starting a new hobby).

The only way to know if your feeling-tones are good guides to well-being is to investigate where they consistently lead. As you begin to label the positive, negative, and neutral feeling-tones that appear in your mind, you will start to notice patterns. Try to determine what triggers them.

Once you've begun to map your emotional circuit breakers, you can open them up and take a look at the wiring. What is it about different people and circumstances that makes you feel the way you do? Is it them? Are they intrinsically amazing or terrible, as the case may be? To what extent do your own beliefs influence your emotional triggers? Slowly, you can begin to organize your life around the things that are good for you, and one at a time weed out the things that are not—some of which may be your own attitudes. I know that has been the case for me.

What's the way to happiness? It's hard to know. Luckily there is a lot of data to use to plot a course. Life is basically a never-ending flood of feedback. In my experience, when I value it for course correction, I'm abler to stay off the rocks (or to get out of shallow waters when I happen to steer into them).

3) "Is this me?"

The next step is to evaluate how your feeling-tones relate to your sense of self. What exactly is your relationship to the instinctive reactions of pleasure or displeasure that arise in you? These are not questions we normally ask. Before I started paying close attention to my emotional reactions, I took it for granted that they said something deeply personal about me; they were an indication of something that could be called the real me.

But now I wonder. The notion of a real me suggests a fixed thing that cannot be changed. It suggests a closed circuit, a locked box. To some extent, it turns automatic impulses into orders that you think you have to follow.

Engaging in this type of mental training challenges such notions. When you consistently identify feeling-tones and then ask "Is this me?", you create a separation between your observing self and the feeling-tone. You become a bird-watcher, identifying and classifying feeling-tones that fly through your mind from a safe distance. This distance allows you a degree of flexibility as to how to translate the feeling-tones into behavior.

If you don't feel an affinity for the question "Is this me?", you can instead ask "Is this mine?" To what extent are you liable for your own unconscious mental reactions? It makes perfect sense to say that we are responsible for our *actions* because they have an effect on the world around us, and (with training) we can learn to change them. But *feeling-tones* are both invisible and entirely involuntary. While you can observe and choose not to act on them (if you have enough presence of mind), you can't keep them from arising in the first place.[3] If you don't think of these feeling-tones as something you voluntarily created, you may feel less obligated to do what they demand. You may also feel less guilt if what they demand isn't so nice.[4]

Summary of the Practice

- Pay attention to feeling-tones of **attraction**, **repulsion**, and **indifference**. Where do you feel them in your body? **Are they permanent**, or do they pass away?
- Begin to notice what **triggers** these feeling-tones. Are there any patterns you can identify? Ask yourself why things appeal to you, repel you, or do nothing at all for you. Is there a compelling reason?
- Question what you believe your feeling-tones say about you as a person. **Are you your feeling-tones**? Or are you just aware of them?

---

3 Though it may be accurate to say that as you learn more about your mental life and the consequences of your actions, what arises may change on its own. Whereas Jack in the Box used to be my favorite restaurant, I no longer feel an urge to drop in for a burger when I drive by (most of the time, at least).

4 In my opinion, releasing guilt for automatic mental events while simultaneously assuming total responsibility for the actions they lead you to perform is a necessary first condition for personal change (which isn't to say that it is sufficient, merely that it's a good place to start).

Your Thoughts

Our thoughts are our most intimate companions. We spend more time with them than with anything else, and you could argue that thoughts are the basis for every good thing humans have made, from uplifting art to suffering-reducing technology.

However, it would be a mistake to suggest that thinking is an uncomplicated source of well-being. If thinking creates works of art and technological innovation, thinking, when unexamined, is also consistently used to justify oppression (think the stigmatization of homosexuals or Jim Crow laws, along with the myriad forms of discrimination extant today), torture (think the Inquisition), and genocide (think the Holocaust). For those with obsessive-compulsive disorder, schizophrenia, and severe depression, thoughts are cruel. Even those of us who don't suffer from mental illness aren't free from the pain of out-of-control thoughts. (Raise your hand if you've never laid awake at night, unable to stop worrying.)

Despite this fact, we tend to ignore the destructive potential of thoughts, choosing instead to focus upon the actual good they do in the world. I think we do this because we are afraid. We recognize that thoughts cause harm, but we don't think there is anything that we can do about it. Thoughts seems so automatic, so entirely out of our hands that turning our attention to their less appealing attributes would just make us depressed, we feel.

While understandable, is this belief also true? At first glance, it seems hard to refute. Policing thoughts can be like throwing gasoline on a fire; punishing people for thoughts that are not deemed appropriate often does little to make them go away (and might actually make them stronger).[5] To a certain extent, thoughts really are automatic. They do simply arise, whether we have asked for them or not,

---

5 See Jonathan Rauch's incisive book *Kindly Inquisitors: The New Attacks on Free Speech* for a thorough (and controversial) argument as to why this may be so.

and neither a government-appointed panel nor a dedicated individual can make them stop.

I would argue that the case isn't open and shut, however. I think you can learn to lessen the harm caused by out-of-control thoughts. In this section, I will present a method for doing so.

It doesn't actually involve doing much of anything, at least not in the traditional sense of doing. The first step is to develop the ability to observe thoughts more clearly. By cultivating a sharper awareness both of the content of thoughts and (even more crucially) the process by which they appear in, move through, and disappear from your mind, you can change the more or less obsessive relationship most of us have with them.

The Practice

How do thoughts work? That question may or may not make sense, depending upon how you interpret it. How do thoughts work on a brain level? I don't know. That's probably not a question that can be answered without incredibly expensive equipment (much of which probably hasn't been developed yet) and a lot more schooling than I will ever have.

Let's refine the question: How do thoughts work in experience? That's more manageable. The only things you need to examine thoughts as you experience them are patience, curiosity, and a couple of helpful questions.

The questions are the same ones we have been using in the other Insight Practices: Is this permanent? Is this an abiding source of well-being? In what sense, if any, is this thought me?

Again, I didn't make up these questions. They come from Buddhist tradition.[6] I don't personally identify as a Buddhist, but I use these questions because they are helpful. There is nothing exclusively Buddhist about them. You don't have to accept a particular worldview to ask them. You are not compelled to come to any particular conclu-

---

6 There are, of course, a large number of Buddhist traditions, but this is not the place to split that hair.

sions. You just have to pay attention to your thoughts and be honest about what you find.

You can choose to ask these questions during a formal practice session (posing them to yourself every time a thought appears), to incorporate them into your everyday life, or to do both. Any time a thought arises is an opportunity to learn something.

1a) "Where did this come from?"

Before I started meditating, I tended to live my life as a mental vagabond, jumping from thought to thought as if they were passing trains. Sometimes that was fun. But sometimes the trains went off the rails. Latching onto every thought that went by was a deeply ingrained habit. It was so automatic that I didn't even notice it. Starting to notice this tendency is the first step to changing it.

One way to begin is to attempt to catch new thoughts as soon as they appear. At first you will probably find it difficult to do this. Thoughts really do come fast and furious, and without practice you will probably experience them as a stream of noise that neither begins nor ends. As your Focus Practice progresses, however, you will probably experience moments that are free of thought. At that point you can prime your attention to wait for one to emerge.

Until you develop that capacity for attention, you can practice following a given thought back to its source. It could be that the pizza you are craving right now is the last link in a chain that was initiated when you walked past a video game store in the mall. The sight of a Wii U reminded you of Mario, which made you think of Italy, which brought the thought of pizza to mind. Maybe you were halfway to the food court without even realizing why you suddenly wanted pizza. How many of the actions you take on a given day are the end result of a chain of thoughts you were totally unaware of? I know this is true of more of my actions than I would like. Stopping to trace the links will help you become more aware of what triggers your thoughts, which may allow you more say over how you translate them into behavior.

1b) "When will this leave?"

If the appearance of thoughts often goes unnoticed, so too does their departure. We wrestle with thought after thought without recognizing the moments at which we have changed partners.

"What's the big deal?" you might think. "I happen to enjoy floating down my stream of consciousness." Sometimes it is fun—until you find yourself chained to an inner tube in a mental squall.

If you're anything like me, even though you *know* that thoughts come and go, you tend to relate to them as if they have always been and will always be. But they haven't, and they won't. Attempting to pay close attention to the point at which a given thought terminates may help you shake the illusion that subsequent thoughts will last forever.

2) "Is this a source of happiness?"

Thoughts powerfully impact our emotional states; compare the excitement that comes from anticipating a vacation to the dread that comes from ruminating upon its end. It's worth reiterating that thinkers throughout history have claimed that happiness and unhappiness are less a direct response to the events of our lives than a result of how we internally respond to them:

> **Hamlet:** "For there is nothing either good or bad, but thinking makes it so."[7]
>
> **The Buddha** (perhaps): "All we are is the result of what we have thought."[8]
>
> **Epictetus**, Stoic philosopher and former Roman slave: "If someone succeeds in provoking you, realize that your mind is complicit in the provocation."[9]
>
> **Marcus Aurelius**, Roman emperor: "You have power over

---

[7] From *Hamlet*, Act 2, Scene 2.
[8] From the *Dhammapada*.
[9] From *The Art of Living: The Classical Manual on Virtue, Happiness, and Effectiveness*.

your mind—not outside events. Realize this, and you will find strength."[10]

Of course, the fact that historical figures like Shakespeare, Marcus Aurelius, and Siddhartha Gautama may have said something doesn't make it true. Anyone can say anything, and anyone can be wrong; as Seneca the Younger, another Stoic philosopher, says about opinions: "The author of the story is a fool, and he who has believed it is a fool as well as he who fabricated it."[11] This practice is about examining your thoughts for yourself, and only then coming to conclusions.

That said, there is evidence that these thinkers are onto something; some compelling research suggests that certain patterns of thought *do* reliably produce suffering. Results from Cognitive Behavioral Therapy—a field that blends cognitive science and psychotherapy—supports this idea.[12] Practitioners have identified a list of **cognitive distortions** that lead people into unhappy places. Do you think you know other people's intentions? If you don't have good evidence, you might be **mind-reading**. Do you have a tendency to ruminate on worst-case scenarios? Perhaps you are **catastrophizing**. Do you often feel that you are personally responsible for the bad moods of others? You might be **personalizing**.

If some patterns of thought may be sources of suffering, does it follow that other patterns of thought may be sources of happiness? Martin Seligman, psychologist and author of *Authentic Happiness: Using the New Positive Psychology to Realize Your Potential for Lasting Fulfillment*, is one of the leading researchers attempting to answer that very question. The research he presents in that particular book relates more immediately to values than to thoughts, but it seems reasonable to believe that prioritizing certain values will impact the type of thoughts you think. Seligman identifies six values that seem to

---

10 From *Meditations*.
11 From *The Tao of Seneca*.
12 See *The Worry Cure* by Robert Leahy for a thorough and practical introduction.

occur across a wide spectrum of human cultures: wisdom and knowledge; justice; courage; love and humility; temperance; spirituality and transcendence (defined as moving beyond narrow self-interest).

Let's make the unfounded assumption that we all know and agree upon what those words mean. What would happen if you deliberately attempted to make those values the foundation of your mental life? Seligman's research suggests that bending your thoughts in these particular directions can have surprising benefits for your daily well-being.

This particular practice, however, is not about attempting to think any specific type of thought; it is about trying to better evaluate the effects of those you already think. "Are you a source of happiness?" You don't have to use those exact words, of course, but if you get into the habit of questioning your thoughts in this way, you will begin to get a clearer picture of how they affect you. With that data in hand, you can plan a more informed way forward.

3) "Is this me?"

You could claim that life is a roughly 75-year search for your self. Many of us take our investigation to the contents of our minds, spending our time panning thoughts for self-nuggets. There are plenty to find, because the mind never shuts up. We live with a narrator in our head, and we take it for granted that that narrator speaks for someone who could be called *me*.

But does it? The question "Is this me?" acts as a wedge between you and your thoughts. What do your thoughts say about you, really? It's not entirely obvious. They say a lot about where you've been, the books you've read, the classes you've taken, the mistakes you've made. They say a lot about your genetics, your life experiences, the dominant beliefs in your society about people who look and sound like you, and your understanding of what all of those things mean.

But none of that is necessarily *you*. I know that my thoughts today are not what they were ten years ago, and they probably won't be the same ten years from now. My thoughts are the product of what I believe about the world, and that will change.

The liberating thing to realize is that thoughts only affect us if we believe they represent us. The power of this practice is in breaking our automatic identification with thoughts. Doing so may free us from the stories they drag us into. We can then choose how to rewrite them.

Summary of the Practice

- Observe the **emergence of thoughts**. Can you detect the moment at which a thought appears in your mind? Notice when one line of thought branches off to a new one. Do you see any patterns? Do any thoughts last forever?
- Note which thoughts are **dead ends**. If you recognize that a given thought is likely to lead you into a downward spiral, you may find yourself able to skip over it. Also pay attention to thoughts that perk you up. Are some thoughts predictable **sources of either happiness or suffering**?
- Question your personal relationship to your thoughts. In what sense **are they you**? In what sense **are they yours**?

Relationships Between Things in the World

This is perhaps the most accessible of the Insight Practices. You will take a closer look at the **relationships** between the people, things, and ideas in the world around you in an attempt to see how they influence one another.

This practice uses a different question than that first three. Rather than asking about impermanence, happiness, and selfhood, you focus on interdependence: "What does this depend upon?" Even if it can be difficult at times, we *are* capable of seeing connections between things. Getting into the habit of consciously looking for them will make it more automatic.

Every interaction is an opportunity to get to the bottom of things. Let's return to the coffee shop to look at human relationships. If the barista doesn't look me in the eye as she hands me my drink, there could be any number of reasons why: maybe her boss just yelled at her; maybe she overheard a coworker gossiping about her; maybe she's stressed about her upcoming organic chemistry final; maybe I smell bad; maybe she spent all morning being hit on and doesn't want to look at another random dude.

Unfortunately, the first thought that jumps into my mind is that she doesn't like me. That doesn't really make any sense because she doesn't know me, but the idea is strangely compelling if I don't examine it. In the language of the cognitive distortions we encountered earlier, I am engaging in **mind-reading**. The reasons why anyone does anything are not as readily apparent as we are primed to think they are. Use those knee-jerk reaction as cues to ask yourself, "What does this depend on?" You'll be much more likely to focus on the other possible rationales for people's actions.

Of course, human relationships aren't the only things that are complicated. Everything in the world is massively and insanely complicated, but we don't always look for that complexity. Explicitly asking yourself, "What does this depend on?" is helpful here as well. The world is too big a picture to see all at once, but sometimes confusion (and the irritation that comes with it) is resolved by actively looking for what depends on what.

Summary of the Practice

- Make a conscious effort to **question your perceptions**. Ask yourself, "What am I missing?" or, "What else is going on here?"
- Look for **interconnections**. What influences what? If you don't know where the wires go, it's hard to tug on them. Use the question, "What does this depend on?" to direct your attention to those connections.

My Struggles with Insight

In some ways, this practice is easier than the Focus Practices because you get to think. If Focus Practices are about sitting still, Insight Practices are about following a trail.

You have questions:
"What does my body actually feel like?"
"What feeling-tone is this?"
"Will this thought last forever?"
"What does that depend on?"

All you have to do is follow those questions wherever they lead.

In other ways, however, this practice is more difficult than the Focus Practices, because the answers to the questions can be unsettling. When I first began to experiment with this practice, I was reasonably comfortable with my view of the world. It wasn't perfect, but it was familiar. This practice, however, asks you to look at familiar things in an entirely unfamiliar way. Probing my body, my feelings, and my thoughts was destabilizing. It started to become clear that I didn't know as much about myself as I thought I did.

Furthermore, I didn't know what to do about that lack of understanding. I saw firsthand that sometimes physical sensations change when I pay attention to them. I learned to recognize that my impulses weren't always helpful. I experienced thoughts as coming and going without any help from me. I saw that it can be very difficult to know what causes what. But I didn't know what it all meant, except that I was really confused.

Suggestions

I think the only way to engage in this practice is to do so very carefully.

I find it helpful to think of myself as a naturalist whose interest is the mind. I mentioned this in the section on feeling-tones, but it's worth returning to. Typical naturalists go into the wild and make detailed observations on the beaks of birds, the shapes of leaves, and the color of bugs.

I think that the only safe way to practice Insight meditation is to observe the mind in the same way. You sample different aspects of subjective experience in an attempt to appreciate what they feel like. Attention is your measuring device. You use it to collect data on your bodily sensations, your instinctive reactions to various stimuli, the mechanical operation of your thoughts, and the connections between things in the world. All you are is a researcher with a pen, marking down what you see.

That might sound sterile, but I don't feel that way. I think it's very useful—and may also be a necessary life-line to keep you tethered to reality. The fact is that, for most of us, subjective experience is surprisingly uncharted territory. When entering the unknown, the danger is in making too much out of what you find. You may find that what you always thought were stable phenomenon change with the simple application of your attention. The impulse is to question what that means.

At times, I've found myself shaken by what I've experienced in meditation. "Wow," I thought, "the Buddhists weren't making this up." The fact that the texts seem to be right about some things made me wonder about others. "If they're not totally wrong about impermanence, what about the other stuff?"

After some painful back and forth[13], I've decided to use the words of astronomer Carl Sagan as a guide for what I'll let myself believe: "Extraordinary claims require extraordinary evidence." I have seen plenty of things fade away, so I'm willing to accept the possibility that any given thing is impermanent[14]. I haven't seen anything get reborn, however. That alone isn't proof that reincarnation doesn't happen, but—given the seemingly improbable metaphysics involved—it would take something pretty spectacular to convince me that it does. I haven't come across anything sufficiently compelling.

Whether you choose to approach belief in the same way is, of course, up to you.

---

13 Painful in part because I was allowing myself to engage in it.
14 Which is not the same as believing that everything is impermanent. The important thing, for me, is to never stop testing. "Is this permanent?" is a question, not an answer.

PRACTICE #3:
Positive Emotion Boosters

SO FAR WE'VE TALKED ABOUT HOW to take control of your attention and then how use it to examine your inner life. In this chapter, we will look at a set of four related practices designed to increase your capacity for positive emotions.

Before we start, however, we need to define our terms. You hear a lot about positivity these days, but it isn't always clear what anyone means by it. For the purposes of this chapter, positivity is an attitude that allows you to accurately identify and then resolve problems.

The world is not perfect. People do suffer: from poverty, injustice, hatred, environmental destruction, sickness, or just the occasional bad-hair day. This approach to positivity allows us to be both realistic and optimistic: realistic because it doesn't turn a blind eye to imperfections;[1] optimistic because of how it responds to them.

Unfortunately, sometimes solutions aren't readily available. The type of positivity I am advocating for recognizes this fact. At times, the act of ruminating upon unsolvable problems is itself the most readily apparent problem. Recognizing when our thinking has strayed into unproductive territory is the first step to redirecting our mental energy to things that can be solved.

A positive attitude, as I have just defined it, won't automatically and immediately save the world, but it may be the best place to start.

That's where the Positive Emotion Boosters come in. They are a set of four exercises designed to fortify your inner life. Practicing them will train the type of thought patterns that are more likely to keep you on your feet when things get tough.

The practices train the following states of mind:[2]

❶ **Goodwill**—genuinely hoping that good things happen to people (yourself included).
❷ **Compassion**—recognizing when someone is in distress and then genuinely wanting to see that stress alleviated.
❸ **Positive Empathy**—a phrase I will use to refer to the capacity to celebrate the happiness of others.
❹ **Poise**—the ability to keep from being too affected by changing circumstances.

Let's take a closer look at how they work.

---

[1] In fact, it actively seeks them out.
[2] There are Sanskrit terms for each of them, but I won't use them. They refer to basic human emotions that I'm sure everyone is familiar with—though if you are interested, you could google either *metta* or *brahmavihara*.

Training Goodwill

You can usually tell when someone wants bad things to happen to you. They probably don't wish you any real harm, but you can tell that it wouldn't bother them if you lost your tennis match, bombed your presentation, or did worse than them on a test. Generally (hopefully?), that person will not be your best friend.

But then other times you come across people who, for some unknown reason, seem to want you to be happy. They ask about your day and really want to hear about it. They cheer you on and mean it, and they celebrate your successes even though there doesn't seem to be anything in it for them. You find yourself gravitating to them for the simple reason that they make you feel good.

It's not surprising. We like to be around people who want us to be happy. I'm calling this state of mind **goodwill**. It's a nice thing to have.

Sometimes it's hard to come by. Sometimes you feel like a world-weary misanthrope who just wants people to go away. We've all been there. It's fine.

I've come to believe that there are things you can do about that, however. This practice is one of those things. It is about making goodwill—for yourself and others—more consistently available. Here's how it works.

The Practice

This practice involves generating mental images of different people and then directing specific messages at them. The messages are crafted to express goodwill. The idea is that generating these sentiments during meditation may make them easier to generate in daily life. With repeated practice, you may be able to shift your emotional baseline in a positive direction, which may cause you to naturally react to people differently. The following is a short list of phrases sometimes taught to English-speakers learning this practice:

"May you be happy."
"May you be free from danger."

"May you have mental well-being."
"May you have physical well-being."
"May you be at ease."

You don't have to use these particular phrases if you don't feel an affinity for them, but I find that they cover the basics of what happiness seems to be: safety, mental and physical health, peace and quiet. The main idea is to come up with a few phrases that communicate your ideas of what happiness is and then to dedicate some time to directing them towards a mental image of others. I like to think of the basic sentiment as a template upon which I can iterate as I see fit. Recently, I have been experimenting with, "May you flourish," which I like.

There is a common list of people you visualize, progressing from those you feel a natural connection for to those who are more distant: yourself; a person you feel very grateful to; a close friend; a neutral person; and finally someone you don't like.

You start out by directing goodwill at yourself for two related reasons. First, you have as much right to well-being as anyone else; and second, it's more difficult to wish others well if you are suffering.[3] If you choose to try this practice, you might want to spend most of your early attempts directing the phrases at yourself. "May I be happy;" "May I be free from danger;" "May I have mental well-being..." et cetera, et cetera.

The next step is to direct the phrases to a person you truly appreciate. In her book on this practice, *Lovingkindness: The Revolutionary Art of Happiness*, Sharon Salzburg[4] recommends selecting a favorite teacher or someone else you have an uncomplicatedly positive relationship with (if such a person exists). She calls this figure a *benefac-*

---

[3] Some say an effective way to ease one's own suffering is to work to ease the suffering of others, which also seems to be true.

[4] Salzburg is a very popular author who (as I understand it) operates largely out of the Theravada school of Buddhism. As I have said, I don't consider myself a Buddhist, but many experienced meditators do. I go to them for tips. *Lovingkindess* is a very clear explication of this practice, and this section is deeply indebted to it.

tor. Get an image of a benefactor in your mind, and direct the phrases at them.

Next, form an image of a close friend and direct the phrases at them.

After that, form an image of someone you don't have any feelings for and send the phrases at that image. Salzburg calls this a *neutral person*. You might select a company receptionist, a local grocery store clerk, or someone else you see but don't have meaningful interactions with.

Finally, form an image of someone you have a difficult time with. This could be a competitor, a critic, a generally offensive person, or someone who has done you personal harm in the past. Direct the phrases at their image.

This practice can be performed as part of a formal meditation session. As Tucker Peck pointed out to me, it does double duty as a Positive Emotion Booster and a Focus Practice, because if you forget to repeat the phrases, then you can't expect your emotions to be boosted. It can also be performed whenever you have a spare moment.

My Struggles with Goodwill

In all honesty, this practice weirded me out at first. It felt a little bit like the kind of self-help advice many (including myself) are most suspicious of: "If you just wish hard enough, you dreams will come true!"

It would be nice if that were the case, but reality seems to be more complicated. So what exactly was the mechanism by which this practice was supposed to work? Were the phrases supposed to literally affect the lives of the people I directed them to? Were they supposed to invoke the help of some supernatural being? Was this basically just "The Secret" masquerading as mental training?

When I thought of the goodwill practice in that light, I really didn't want to do it.

Suggestions

As I tried to make clear in the initial description of this practice, I did eventually find a way to conceptualize it as something worth doing. The work of Richard Davidson, a neuroscientist who runs the Center for Investigating Healthy Minds at the University of Wisconsin-Madison, provided the key.

Davidson researches the physiological effects of meditation upon the brain. He presents a summary of that research in his book (authored with Sharon Begley), *The Emotional Life of Your Brain,* and while I am not qualified to do the research justice (though I highly recommend the book to those who are interested), my main takeaway was that, in principle, the type of repetitive mental stimulation involved in meditative practices *can* actually have demonstrable physiological effects on the brain. In other words, repeating phrases over and over again might actually do something to you.

From this perspective, this practice (in fact all four of the practices in this section) can be thought of as a flight simulator for certain emotions. If you think of thoughts as underpinned by patterns of neural firing, it is not unreasonable to think that those patterns could be rearranged.

At this point, we don't have the capability to download new thought patterns straight to our brains. The only way to change the way we think is the old fashioned way: through repetition. This practice is about rewriting your attitudes one thought at a time.

When I recite these phrases, I don't do it because I think anyone is listening. I don't do it because I think anyone else is soothed by the things I repeat in my own mind. Sometimes I can soothe myself, however, and there is reason to believe that repeating the phrases also affects my brain.

It is a painstaking process. Your thought patterns won't change immediately (at least mine haven't). There is reason to believe, however, that change is inexorable. Little by little, the faces of your benefactors, your friends, random people you've never spoken to, and maybe even people you don't like may trigger feelings of goodwill.

At least, that's the idea. In practice, even after training, goodwill may only be there if you reach for it. In my mind, the training is worth doing if it can bring goodwill onto a lower shelf.

> **Summary of the Practice**
>
> - Select a **series of phrases** (generally less is more) to communicate a wish for the **well-being** of others. If you like, you can use, "May you be happy," "May you have mental well-being," "May you have physical well-being," and "May you be at ease." You could also try, "May you flourish."
> - Direct the phrases at yourself. Then, direct them at the images of people who are progressively more distant from you. You can experiment with this order: benefactor, close friend, neutral person, someone who causes you some degree of distress.

Training Compassion

Human beings suffer. That's not the only thing we do, of course, but it is certainly one of our main activities. Given that fact, it's worth figuring out a constructive way to respond to suffering. If there is a single, most effective way to respond to any and all types of suffering, I don't know what it is. My intuition is to say that there is no such thing. Genuinely wanting to alleviate suffering, however, seems like a useful first step.

This practice is about getting more familiar with what that feels like.

The Practice

This practice follows the same general format as the practice for training goodwill. Select a phrase intended to generate a particular sentiment, and then direct that sentiment at mental images of people you relate to in different ways. The classic phrase for training compassion is, "May you be free of suffering." Again, I don't think it really matters exactly what you say as long as a) you remember to say it, and b) what you say expresses the basic sentiment you're going for.

This particular phrase does two things. First, it forces you to recognize that suffering exists. People are suffering all of the time, but if you're anything like me, then you mostly ignore it. Once you've noticed suffering, this phrase prompts you to respond to it in a helpful way. In this tradition, a helpful way to respond is with a heartfelt, visceral sense of wanting to take the suffering away.

The practice traces the same expanding circle as the previous one. Pretend that you're in a flight simulator, activating different brain regions in order to make them fire more easily in the future. Start by directing the thought-loop at yourself: "May I be free of suffering."

Continue by increasing the radius of your concern. Imagine your benefactor having a tough time. Alternatively, if there are any children in your life, you might imagine consoling one of them on a rough day. We're wired in such a way that it is very easy to feel compassion for children. You might as well use that to your advantage.

After that, imagine a close friend having a tough time: "May you be free of suffering."

Next, a person you don't really know: "May you be free of suffering."

Finally, you can direct the phrase towards a person you don't like: "May you be free of suffering, jackass who cut me off on the freeway this morning." "May you be free of suffering, unreasonable and vindictive boss."[5] Or, if you're feeling particularly charitable, "May you be free of suffering, convicted murderer."

Maybe it's crazy, but I get the feeling that the difficult people in the world need this more than anyone else. Maybe they are just people in possession of a lot of pain that they don't know what to do with. Maybe the first thing we can do to help is recognize that.

Even if that's true, this practice won't help them very much, at least

---

5 For all the bosses out there: "May you be free of suffering, uncommitted and irresponsible employee."

not directly. This is a training exercise for *you*. The point is to help you access a compassionate state of mind when you need it. Other people benefit when they meet you because you become abler to help them.

My Struggles with Compassion

You'd think training compassion would be easy: "Compassion? I'm a good person, I can do that."

But it's not easy, or at least it hasn't been for me. I have two main difficulties: I feel weird directing compassion at myself; and I have trouble knowing what to do about the suffering I recognize in others.

May I Be Free of Suffering (?)

There are two ways to say this phrase. One way is as a declarative statement: "May I be free of suffering." This basically says, "I am in favor of a world in which I suffer less."

But you can also ask it as a question: "May I be free of suffering?" In other words, "Is it really OK for me not to suffer?" Somewhat perversely, when I do this practice, I find myself asking the question a lot, and I don't always have a clear answer.

What percentage of the punishment we experience in life is self-inflicted? Some might be tempted to say none, but in my experience that isn't the case. Maybe I'm just crazy and/or very privileged, but the vast majority of punishment I suffer comes at my own hands. I could always be better. I could always try harder. I could always do more. In the past I've often punished myself for my limitations.

I think that the quest for constant improvement is good. It can be a powerful source of both well-being and meaning. I'm starting to think that self-punishment isn't the best way to pursue it, however.

Your Suffering Is My Suffering?

When I first started this practice, I tricked myself into thinking that relieving everyone's suffering was my responsibility. I started to notice that people were unhappy a lot of the time. Their unhappiness struck me—very bizarrely—as a sign of my own failure. This is crazy. But it's also a feeling that's hard to shake at times.

Suggestions

I think I've hit on some solutions to my problems. Both of them involve looking at myself from a more realistic perspective.

Why Not Me?

As I sat in my room repeating the thought, "May you be free of suffering," I kept encountering the same resistance: "You don't deserve to be free of suffering!"

It was a strong thought; it was an embarrassing thought. I wished it wasn't there, but that didn't make it go away.

I decided to examine it. Why, exactly, was this thought appearing in my mind? Asking myself this dredged up all sorts of interesting and painful things. A litany of my past mistakes and personal weaknesses began to parade through my mind. Looking at them made the rationale for my resistance clear: "Only perfect people deserve to be free of suffering, and you are not perfect."

"Hmm," I thought, after eventually admitting that I was, in fact, beholden to that belief. "Let's dig deeper." I let myself think about what was sustaining that belief.

I eventually realized that I thought the belief was helping me. The logic went something like this: "If I punish myself long enough for not being perfect, maybe someday I will be." This belief was like a software program running in the background of my mind. It had been playing for most of my life, influencing the way I interacted with myself, with my tasks, and with other people, but I had never really noticed it.

Once I became aware of it, however,[6] I felt that I needed to evaluate how reasonable it was.

---

6 And stopped trying to deny its presence.

Is it reasonable to think that everyone who isn't perfect should suffer? To put it another way, if it was in my power, would I willingly inflict suffering on those who have made mistakes in their life? Or would I give them a break? I like to think I would give them a break, at least in my best moments. Is there any reason not to treat myself the same way?

I can't think of a good one.

Unless, of course, beating myself up *would* actually make me better in the long run. I decided to look as closely as I could at the effects of being hyper-critical of myself. Did it make me a better person? I realized that while it's hard to pin down exactly what makes someone good, it's useful to start with good qualities. People can certainly express what we understand to be good qualities, such as kindness, honesty, courage, fairness, and the like. Is it reasonable to believe that those qualities will develop as the result of self-flagellation?

I think the answer is no.

In sum, I don't see a reason why I deserve to suffer anymore than anyone else does, and I don't see how punishing myself would help me develop positive qualities. My own suffering doesn't seem to do anyone any good. In fact, it seems that I am a lot more helpful when I'm *not* in suffering. When I think about it that way, I feel more comfortable striving to be free(r) of it.

Avoiding Burn-Out

Once you've become more comfortable managing your own suffering, you can turn your attention to the suffering of others. This requires a slightly different set of skills, because you can't relate to the suffering of others in the same way that you can to your own. Your own suffering is more immediate both in terms of your ability to feel it and your ability to do something about it. You have access to your own emotional state, and you have access to the circumstances in your life that could be influencing those states. To the extent that your pain is a result of your attitudes, you can do the work necessary to change them (even if it takes a while).

By contrast, you don't know the intimate details of the mental lives of others. Unless you know someone very well, it's difficult to pinpoint exactly what is getting them down. Even assuming you did know exactly why someone feels bad, and also knew exactly what would make them feel better, you can't force them to make those changes. Any attempt to do so would probably have perverse[7] results.

So what's a would-be caring person to do? How does one attend to the suffering of those around them in a way that doesn't actually make things worse? To start, let's investigate the actual experience of compassion and then look at when it is appropriate to act on that feeling. After that, I'd like to mention a primary impediment to compassion that I have discovered in myself, plus roads that seem to lead around it.

Feeling the Pain vs. Feeling Bad About It

Compassion is a word you hear a lot, but it isn't one that is often clearly defined. It's related in some way to empathy, which is often defined as the ability to sense another person's feelings, experiences, and pain as if they were your own. Ideally, this creates a connection between you and that person, which would cause you to act in such a way as to ease that pain (if possible). It is that connection combined with the resulting visceral impulse to help that we can call compassion.

Recognizing suffering doesn't inevitably engage this process, of course. Sometimes being connected to someone in their pain—rather than resulting in the desire to help—results in the desire to cut the connection. Sometimes we experience the pain of others as a personal affront. We may read it as a sign that we ourselves are bad people. I feel this way almost every time I pass a homeless person. I feel horrible that circumstances have brought him or her a piece of cardboard while simultaneously bringing me a whole lot of nicer things. I feel guilty that I can't/don't do more to help. This feels very bad, so usually I just put my head down and walk away. This, perhaps, is what happens when you have empathy (an awareness of the existence of pain) without compassion (a personal connection that evokes a wish to help).[8]

---

7 "Perverse" meaning to have the opposite result of what was intended.
8 The particular words "empathy" and "compassion" aren't really pegged to

Of course, appropriately responding to the suffering of the homeless and other disadvantaged people is significantly complicated by the logistical difficulties of offering meaningful assistance, which makes evaluating an appropriate response somewhat complicated. For now, let's look at how to get from empathy to compassion. I find it helpful to first remove my sense of self from the situation. It's possible to sense suffering without necessarily feeling responsible for having caused it. People suffer for a lot of different reasons, and most of them have nothing (directly) to do with me. If I happen to be standing on someone's foot, there is a relatively easy way to fix that problem. If, however, my neighbor contracts a neurodegenerative disorder, I probably don't want to feel responsible for that.

What I can do is recognize someone's pain and then offer my concern. To a certain extent, I think that's all compassion is. I suffer. You suffer. We all suffer. In that way, we're all the same. When we're able to connect with others in this way, the desire to make their suffering go away may arise on its own. You may not be able to actually make their suffering go away, but you might be able to avoid piling more suffering on top of it. I think this leads us to an important concern: knowing when to back off.

When Trying to Help Is Hurting

Suffering is tenacious and its causes aren't always obvious. Barging into someone's life with little more than good intentions is more likely to cause harm than good—both to the person you're trying to help and to yourself. (It's not fun to have your altruistic offers rejected or abused.)

This can be a difficult pill to swallow, and it will probably stick in your throat until you accept it. Once you have, the question becomes, "What *can* you do with your compassion?" I think you can use it as a drive to learn more about people and why they do the things they do. When you care, you'll be more willing to look closely at why people

---

anything, so it's possible that I'm using them differently than you might. It's the underlying mental states that I'd like you to draw your attention to.

suffer. Then, when you have a clearer picture of those causes, you may be abler to take actions that help. In some cases, the right action might be going away.

A Barrier to Compassion

In attempting to do this practice, I have noticed certain attitudes that make it harder for me to feel compassionate towards others (and myself). The primary barrier I find is a tendency to judge whether I think someone's suffering is warranted. This is a largely unconscious calculus, and I have to pay close attention to catch it happening. "You reap what you sow." "You get what you deserve." "You brought it upon yourself." These are all things we say when we think people deserve their suffering. We tend to look for reasons to reserve our sympathy. We're social animals, and punishment of what we deem anti-social behavior is a deeply ingrained, almost entirely automatic process.

And yet I'm not convinced that it's always helpful. It's possible that punishment is sometimes necessary to show that a given behavior is unacceptable, but at other times punishment might just make the behavior worse. A commitment to compassion—to reasoning with the well-being of one's self and others as a primary concern—may give you the ability to pause in challenging situations. In that pause, you are more free to deliberate upon the benefits of alternative responses.

Summary of the Practice

- Choose a **phrase** that helps you access **compassion**. You can start with, "May you be free of suffering." The idea is to choose something that quickly connects you to a person in pain and gets you feeling for them.
- Imagine **people in pain**. Start with yourself, then think of someone very close to you (maybe a child, grandchild, niece, or nephew). Move to a close friend, then to a person you barely know, and finally to someone who gives you problems. "May you be free of suffering," you can say to them. Maybe you won't feel anything. That's probably normal (at least I hope it is, for my sake). Attitudes change slowly.

Training Positive Empathy

What I'm calling positive empathy[9] is the ability to revel or at least share in other people's happiness.

You'd think that this would also be easy, but the fact that I couldn't easily come up with a word for it may be telling. Maybe we don't prioritize it so much as a culture. Strangely, we *do* have a word for reveling in other people's suffering, even if it is borrowed from the Germans. I won't deny that sometimes *schadenfreude* can be appealing, but if there is another side to that coin, we might do well to develop it.

And there is another side. It's clearly possible to be happy for other people when they succeed. If it weren't, celebrations would suck. Unfortunately, this sense of taking joy in other people's accomplishments isn't always readily available. Being happy for friends and family when they do well is easier than feeling happy for strangers or people you don't like. But even then, are we always truly happy for the people we care about when they do well? I wish I could say I was, but if I'm being honest, sometimes all I get is jealous.

What, exactly, is the point of jealousy? Presumably, each of our emotions developed for a specific social purpose.[10] Jealousy seems to be related to social position. When we feel that someone is moving up the social ladder—and, more importantly, faster than we are—jealousy may be our mind's way of trying to cut them down to size.

There may have been an environment in which this behavior was adaptive, but I don't think we live there anymore. The fact is that there is enough happiness to go around, and jealousy serves only to hide it from view.

In thinking about whether or not jealousy is a positive force in our lives, we have to consider more than just what it does; we also have to think about what it prohibits. What are the opportunity costs of

---

9 I thought I had made this term up, but it appeared in a Google search my editor ran so I can't claim credit for it.
10 Or a handful of them.

jealousy? If I wasn't feeling jealous of my neighbor's new car (or whatever, I don't actually care about cars), what could I be feeling instead?

I could be feeling positive empathy. If you're happy, I'm happy. That's the attitude. Everyone knows what that feels like. This practice is about learning to feel it more often. Because, frankly, jealousy sucks.

The Practice

"May your happiness increase."

That's the general idea behind the phrase for this practice. When someone is happy, can you delete your own feelings of inadequacy and just feel good for them? This gets harder depending on the person in question, but I'd love to be able to feel this way all of the time.

Before you start imagining happy people, however, first imagine a happy you. Recall a time that something good happened to you—or that you did something good for someone else. "May my happiness increase," you can say. Personally, I say, "May my good qualities increase."

Next, imagine that something amazing has happened to someone you love. Imagine that your child (or your nephew or your cousin) got an "A" on a math test, or that your partner just found the cure for cancer. Try to imagine the joy on their face. They just did something amazing! "May your happiness increase," you say.

Next, imagine a close friend celebrating a similarly invigorating success. She's walking down the aisle! He just found out that he's about to be on *Iron Chef*! "May your happiness increase," you say.

Then, choose someone you don't really have any relationship with. Did you hear that Jim in HR won the lottery? Wow! I can barely remember what you look like, Jim in HR, but, "May your happiness increase."[11]

Finally, imagine that something really good happened to someone you don't like. Google offered to buy your business competitor? Your high-school rival is posting on Facebook about her MD? That team you hate just won the World Series? In these situations, my knee-jerk

---

[11] Given what sometimes happens to people who win the lottery, Jim might need this more than you'd think.

reaction is to get annoyed: "I wanted the Mariners to win the World Series, dammit!"

But deep down, the people you don't like are all just people. They're exactly like you. You want to do well, so why shouldn't they? Form an image of them celebrating. At first it will probably feel like someone is stomping on your heart. That's fine. "May your happiness increase," you say. Even if it's grudging at first, eventually you may find that it gets better. People you once saw as mortal enemies might start to look like normal people.

My Struggles with Positive Empathy

We may not be predisposed to spread the positive empathy. The impulse to compete is baked into our DNA. We want to get ours, which means that sometimes we want others to not get theirs. And luckily so. Competition really does drive innovation. We get better when we are pushed.

But competition isn't always healthy.

Some fights are friendly, while others are to the death: business deals, divorce trials, bar fights, and tennis matches come to mind. If I'm playing a tennis match, how can I be happy for my opponent when he aces me? If I'm applying for a job, how can I be happy for the person who beats me out? And how about serial killers? Do I want *their* happiness to increase, too?

Suggestions

There are two things that have made positive empathy a little bit more accessible to me than it used to be. The first is the recognition that I don't have a greater right to happiness than anyone else (or vice versa). The second is the realization that denying people happiness, or otherwise resenting it, tends to make my life worse than if I celebrated it.

Who Do I Think I Am?

You could make the claim—and I am—that we come more or less programmed to look after ourselves. Our thinking patterns appear to selectively preference information most relevant to our personal concerns (and those of groups we identify with). The upshot is that we tend to see ourselves as the center of the universe: "How will this affect *me*?" we wonder. "What does this mean for *my* life?" We are certainly capable of thinking about others, but even then the most significant others are those whom we see as relevant to ourselves.

This line of thinking often comes with lamentations about human selfishness. I won't deny having traveled down those roads in the past, but I no longer think that our bias for self-interest is something to try and dispense with. I'm not even sure that such an attempt is comprehensible. Maybe an organism not endowed with a healthy sense of self-interest would either die immediately or be such a burden on its compatriots that it would be a source of constant resentment. If you don't look after yourself, then you become someone else's obligation. Maybe it's actually good to think of yourself first.

If this is the case, it's helpful to remember that everyone else probably has a similar orientation. Even those who engage in self-destructive behavior probably focus more on their sense of self than on others—it just so happens that they think that self is somehow "bad" and needs to be punished.

Most of us engage in self-destructive behavior at different points in our lives, but probably more often than not, we want to win. Yes, I want to get every job I apply for. Yes, I want to ace my opponent on every point. Yes, I want to win the lottery.

But so does everyone else; and they have every right to feel that way. From this perspective, it is reasonable for me to want to win, while refusing to deny anyone else their right to do the same. If you beat me, good on you.[12]

Pragmatic Selflessness

I want to be as happy as I possibly can at all times. Why wouldn't I? The thing is, one of the biggest stumbling blocks to my own happiness is an inability to allow other people theirs. When you begrudge people success, from their perspective you become an obstacle. When faced with an obstacle, people want to remove it. This means that when you begrudge people happiness, you shouldn't be surprised if they fight you.

Life isn't fun when people are trying to remove you from it. Luckily, I think there's something you can do about that. If you cheer people on instead of fighting them, they'll want you around. When people want you around, you'll probably be happy. The logic is simple.

In fact, it is already quite well-mapped by academics. Game theory is a field that attempts to tease out what happens when multiple actors compete for things. It identifies three main games, or patterns of interaction. The worst of all possible games is the *negative-sum game*. In a negative sum-game, both parties come out worse than when they went in. (An acrimonious shouting match between romantic partners comes to mind.)

The next kind of game is the *zero-sum game*. In a zero-sum game, there is a clear winner and a clear loser. Winning entails taking possession of some resource that can't be shared, which creates haves and have-nots. Many human activities are played as zero-sum games, including athletic contests, corporate advancement, and traditional competitions for natural resources.

And yet, just because we conceive of something as a zero-sum game doesn't mean it must be played as one. When my editor Wes Matlock read this passage, he made the following comment: "Happiness doesn't have to be a zero-sum game." You could make the argument

---

12 I have to admit that wanting to win is easier for me in some fields than others. It has something to do with my personal perceived right to win, which is different depending upon the environment. It might be that this practice will bring many such limiting beliefs to light. I'm working on a number of mine.

that happiness *can't* be a zero-sum game. As long as you are actively trying to crush someone's dreams, you may—at least unconsciously—suffer the psychological backlash of your ill will. That is perhaps a stronger claim than I can reasonably make here, but I could make a leaner one: there is a limit to the happiness that can be won in zero-sum games.

That brings us to the third class of game identified by game theory: *positive-sum games*. In a positive-sum game, both parties benefit from participation. In his book *Non-Zero: The Logic of Human Destiny*, the amateur scholar Robert Wright makes the bold but well-researched claim that the arc of history tells the story of expanding positive-sum games. Starting with the transition from single- to multi-cellular organisms and moving through biological time to our interconnected human present, Wright argues that progress can be measured by the degree to which actors in any given environment can transition from the cutthroat logic of zero-sum to the cooperative, mutually beneficial logic of positive-sum.

As is clear to any student of history, this transition is not smooth, and our penchant for drawing boundaries around in-group and out-group members has caused (and continues to cause) horrible tragedies, including but not limited to rape, slavery, and genocide. Those tragedies may be the logical consequence of conceptualizing happiness as a zero-sum game.

It may be that the only way out is to rethink the games we are playing. It may be that the best way to maximize your happiness is to fold as many other people into it as possible.

Also, don't worry about serial killers. Leave them to the FBI.

Summary of the Practice

- Select a **phrase** like, "May your happiness increase." As long as it gets you in the habit of **responding positively to the happiness of others**, it's good.

Summary of the Practice (cont.)

- Imagine **a series of people** in various **celebratory moments**. Start with yourself. From there, progress to someone very easy to be happy for, to a close friend, to someone you barely know. Close out, if you dare, with somebody who you wouldn't normally wish good things upon. This will probably feel stupid, but abilities grow only when they're stretched.
- Reflect upon the fact that everyone else feels as important to themselves as you do to yourself. Is your right to happiness any greater (or lesser) than anyone else's?

Training Poise

Poise is—I think—what we call the state of being unfazed by things. More often than not, we ride life like a roller coaster. We go up, we go down, we spin around. Life isn't exactly like a roller coaster, however. When you're on a roller coaster, you can be reasonably sure that you won't fall off; life, unfortunately, doesn't come with safety inspectors.

And there's no way to remedy that. There are no guarantees. Maybe you *are* in the process of plunging to your death. It happens. Poise is having the clarity of mind to grab the side of the ride as you fall. Poise is the squirrel suit you use to glide to safety. Poise is the safety net that catches you before you hit the ground and splatter into a million bloody bits.

Poise is a very underrated skill. When you've got your roots deep in it, life won't be able to blow you around. You'll be a willow that bends and snaps right back up. This particular practice is about familiarizing yourself with that state so that when the shit really does hit the fan, you'll be nimble enough to keep from getting covered in it.

The Practice

"This is not my universe."

I learned this phrase from Tucker Peck, who in turn learned it from Sharon Salzburg. What does it have to do with keeping your cool?

Well, first you have to ask yourself when you lose your cool. Generally, I lose my cool when I'm trying to control things that are fundamentally beyond my control, for example when I'm late to class (I'm a teacher), or my PowerPoint presentation won't open, or my tennis players are running around hitting balls at each other (I'm also a tennis coach). In these situations, things aren't going the way I think they should, and this knocks me off my rocker.

But does it have to? It's unclear how the world could ever operate precisely as I want it to. How much control do we really have over the forces we live with? Can we control weather patterns? No. Can we control traffic patterns? No. Can we control neural firing patterns in other people's brains? No. The worlds we live in are composed of countless actors doing exactly what they've been conditioned to do. A lot of that is entirely out of our hands.

Which doesn't mean, luckily, that we can't do anything about it. It just means that we would be smart to plan our responses in ways that are more likely to achieve the effects we want. Sometimes it works better to go with the grain than against it. Sometimes you have to use a little bit of judo to tip the world in the direction you'd like it to go.

You can't do that if you're too busy fuming. I use "This is not my universe" to remind myself how small I really am. It reminds me exactly how many systems I am embedded in. It disrupts my chimpanzee-derived[13] notions of how much control I have over the world. It dispels the fog of frustration to reveal the maze (or at least parts of it) that we all live in.

Take a seat and repeat the phrase to yourself: "This is not my universe." It may make you more aware of the things that are not under your control—which may in turn alert you to the things that actually are. Take care of those.

You can follow the same protocol as the other three practices. Imagine someone very dear to you. Imagine them protesting against forces that are outside of their control. "This is not your universe."

Imagine a close friend in the same situation. "This is not your universe."

---

13 Well, pre-chimpanzee, really.

Imagine a neutral person and then someone you don't care for. "This is not your universe."

Whose universe is this, really? Nobody's, I guess. Not mine, certainly. As long as I keep that in mind, it irritates me less when the universe doesn't behave the way I want it to. That in turn frees me up to engage with it in more constructive ways.

My Struggles With Poise

My struggles with this practice can also be broken down into two categories: confusion about what poise actually means, and defeat at the hands of impossible standards.

Poise or Apathy?

Sometimes I have a tough time differentiating between poise and apathy. I originally took poise to be the state of not caring about anything. "If I don't care about anything," I reasoned, "then nothing can bother me!"

I experimented with that for a while. But if that's what poise is, it's hard to say why you would want it. Caring about things—in the sense of aspiring for their improvement—is a great source of positive energy. Not caring about anything leads to evenings on the couch with a bag of potato chips. Boring.

Violently Calming Yourself Is an Oxymoron

Sometimes, I can be pretty dumb. When I first started getting into the idea of poise,[14] I came to think that it was better to be relaxed than to be agitated. In general, I think that's probably true.

But the word "better" is tricky. When you think "poise, good; agitation, bad", you may get agitated by the fact that you're agitated. I did. When I found myself getting agitated, I berated myself. "You're sup-

---

14 Which, if you read other meditation books on this practice, you will find translated as "equanimity."

posed to be calm!" I've sometimes said, "It's better!"

This reaction, of course, is not calming. It makes me more agitated, which makes me even more annoyed. I soon find myself struggling against a cascade of self-recrimination that terminates in a splitting headache.

Suggestions

Redefining Poise

Poise—as I now understand it—isn't so much "not caring about anything" as it is "not allowing yourself to get too carried away by anything." You don't go manic with excitement, and you don't fall into pits of despair. You feel calm, comfortable, and capable of handling pretty much anything. Poise is energizing. Poise is engaged. Poise allows you to look life in all of its shifty eyes without blinking or looking away.

Apathy, by contrast, is what it feels like to be dead. I think a good rule to live by is: "Don't be dead until you die."

Rethinking "Better"

Is it "better" to be relaxed than agitated? If so, what exactly is better about it?

Well, when you're agitated you won't be able to think clearly, which means you won't be able to solve problems. You might say or do things that you later regret, which will create problems. Problems are annoying, and the whole point of these practices (at least as far as I see them) is to get better at fixing problems, not to make more of them.

I've found that the most effective way for me to maintain poise is to continually remind myself what I want to do with it. Poise is useful because it provides a stable foundation for intelligent, helpful, reasoned action. Reimagining poise as a springboard for action makes it easier for me to return to when I get thrown off. Maybe the same will be true for you.

> **Summary of the Practice**
> - Choose a phrase that reminds you **what is and isn't under your control**. I like "This is not my universe." The point isn't to feel helpless. Rather, it's to recognize that helplessness arises when you take on forces that are beyond you.
> - Take some time to repeat the phrase. Follow the **same progression** we have followed in the other practices (person near and dear to you, close friend, neutral person, and person you don't like). Form an image of each and say, "This is not your universe"—because it isn't.

A Final Word

I should stress that I'm not very good at this. I'm not a constantly brimming fountain of goodwill. I ignore suffering as much as I attend to it. I do compare and compete in destructive ways at times,[15] and I'm not always able to keep calm and carry on. But I am a little bit *more* capable of all of these things than I was when I started the practice. An upward trend is all I'm looking for.

And an Important Caveat

There is another pitfall I feel compelled to point out before moving on. While these practices could be viewed as a way of training mental states that promote cooperation, that very fact could make you vulnerable to manipulation. This has been true for me. While I think it is important to approach interpersonal interactions with a constructive, positive-sum frame of mind, it's worth noting that some people will

---

15 I'll reiterate that I'm not claiming that competition is bad, merely that it can get out of hand. See Po Bronson and Ashley Merriman's *Top Dog: The Science of Winning and Losing* for a thorough discussion of the reasons to keep competition as a personal value.

not do the same.

It has been my experience that some people have a much more zero-sum mindset. They will try to take as much as they can from you, while giving as little as possible in return. In these situations, if you neglect your own interests, you will be taken advantage of.

How do you know if your attempts at cooperation will be reciprocated or abused? In his book *Give and Take: Why Helping Others Drives Our Success*, Adam Grant, a professor at the Wharton School of Business, presents research on something called *reciprocity styles*. He identifies three main styles: *givers*, who try to give more than they get; *matchers*, who give when the other party seems likely to give back; and *takers*, who rarely give at all, focusing instead on maximizing their own returns while minimizing contributions.

Upon reading about these styles, my first impulse was to jump to the giver orientation. "If you're a good person," I thought, "then obviously you would want to be a giver."

The truth is more complicated. Grant points out that there are actually two types of givers, and one of them is wide-open to manipulation by takers. What Grant calls *selfless givers*—people who reflexively expect that everyone will reciprocate their generosity— often end up being taken advantage of. They become a source of free resources for takers (and even some matchers) to parasitize. To make matters worse, selfless givers (whom we could also call indiscriminate givers) feel obligated to keep giving, even as they are sucked dry.

The problem with selfless givers is that they never revise their expectations of others. They give and give, even to people who use them.

The case for generosity is not hopeless, however. Grant points to a different class of giver, one that is much more difficult to manipulate; the *otherish giver*. Otherish givers are more free with their generosity than matchers (who usually like to be sure that their favors will be returned before offering them), but are always on the lookout for takers. When an otherish giver recognizes a taker, he or she disengages quickly. This allows the otherish giver to maximize opportunities for positive-sum interactions without being used by those playing zero-sum games.

I'm starting to think that it's useful to go into most interactions assuming that the other party is a matcher. Matchers respond very well to givers, as they know that interacting with them will be beneficial. Assuming that you're interacting with a matcher will allow you to be generous. It's vital, however, to reevaluate based upon how the person reacts to your generosity. If they respond as a matcher or a giver, then you've probably found a productive relationship. If, however, they respond as a taker, then your best bet is to (politely and amicably, if possible) cut ties with them.[16]

---

16 See Grant's book for much more detail on reciprocity styles, including ways to recognize takers.

PRACTICE #4:

Visualizations

SO FAR WE'VE TALKED ABOUT a number of ways to both train and use your attention. In this final section, we'll discuss one more: how focusing on mental imagery can positively impact your immediate state of mind.

If you read almost any book on meditation, you'll quickly notice how rich the imagery is: your mind is the sky; your mind is a stage; your mind is a deep and expansive ocean.

This imagery is for more than just decoration: you can use it to change your mood.

I'll describe some of the imagery that appears in the contemplative texts I've read, which includes images of **water**, **fire**, and **light**. I'll briefly discuss the ways in which focusing upon them may shift your mood in a positive direction. Then I'll share the way in which some basic images from **computing** have clarified the way I relate to the process of thinking.

The Practice

Water Images

The mind is often likened to water. It makes sense. The more you pay attention to your mind, the more it feels like something that flows—or doesn't, as the case may be. Sometimes my mind moves like a river; sometimes it settles into a puddle. The river is clear, but the puddle is full of parasites.

Some meditation manuals describe the cumulative effects of consistent practice with water images. They say that the mind can be experienced as:

- **a waterfall**
- **a rushing river**
- **a calm lake**
- **a vast, quiet ocean**

Rather than literally picturing a body of water in my mind, I try to relate to the current quality of my mental experience as if it were water. For example, sometimes thoughts seem to pound you like a waterfall. This can be painful, but it's worth remembering that some people stand under waterfalls because they find it refreshing. What happens if you treat your thoughts as a massage, rather than as torture implements?

Once you have the association between thought and water firmly in your mind, you may find that shifting the type of water image—for example from a waterfall to a glassy lake—may also change the quality of your thoughts. It works for me.

Fire Images

Fire is not neutral. It burns down houses or it purges the forest of dead wood. When your mind is out of control, it can feel like your brain is burning down. At that point, you'd do well to reach for a fire extinguisher.

But a controlled burn can be very useful. Keying images of fire into your mind may clear away any creepers that are choking it.

Sometimes fire gets me out of bed in the morning. You know that moment when the alarm clock goes off? You open your eyes and think, "Dammit."

That was how I used to wake up. It still is, sometimes. I'm experimenting with a different method, however. As soon as I open my eyes,

I sometimes imagine a spark going off. I then imagine that the spark catches, burning away all of cords tying me to sleep. If I time it right, I find myself out of bed and in the kitchen brewing coffee before I have a chance to complain. Sometimes I don't time it right. It's hard to get out of bed on those mornings. The good thing is that there's always the next morning to try again.

Thoughts that hold me back aren't restricted to the moment just after I wake up, of course. They pop up all of the time. Reasons why I'm not good enough to do something. Reasons why something isn't worth my time. Reasons why I'll do it later. I feel like I can tell which of these are legitimate concerns and which are excuses. I try to heed the warnings and torch the bullshit.

It turns out that bullshit starts a good fire.

Light Images

Light is perhaps the most evocative image we have. It stands for understanding. It stands for wisdom. It stands for goodness. Images of light are so ubiquitous that sometimes they come across as either hokey or manipulative.

And yet, I've found that images of light do get my spirits up.

In his book *Why Meditate? Working with Thoughts and Emotions*, French monk Matthieu Ricard describes a practice called *tonglen*. It uses mental images of light to clear away thoughts you'd rather not have. Imagine your unpleasant thoughts and feelings as smoke, Ricard says. With every in-breath, draw that smoke into a ball of piercing white light at your chest. Imagine the smoke disappearing into it. With every out-breath, imagine beams of that same light shooting through your body, conducted along your bones, blasting through your brainstem, pooling at your fingertips.

"That's kind of weird," I thought. But then I tried it. And it kind of works. There is an intuitive similarity between negative emotions and smoke. When you're down on yourself or the world around you, your inner life does feel obscured by something like smoke or smog. The practice of *tonglen* can have the effect of clearing away that smog. When I allow myself to cycle through a few rounds of it, I generally feel refreshed.

You can use *tonglen* on other people as well. Find someone who is clearly having a rough time. Suck in their unpleasant thoughts (in your imagination, obviously), transform them into light, and breathe out. Watch the light settle on their shoulders like snow.

This won't do anything for them[1] but it may help you relate to their struggles in a more constructive way. Seen from this perspective, *tonglen* is closely related to the practice for training compassion we encountered in the section on Positive Emotion Boosters. Whereas that practice uses a verbal cue ("May you be free of suffering") to train compassion, this one uses a visual cue. The methods are different, but the underlying mental state is very similar.

Concepts from Computing

I don't know a lot about computers. I do know that—structurally—brains and computers work differently. One is made of carbon and uses both electricity and chemicals to convey internal messages, whereas the other is made of silicon and uses only electrons.[2]

But, functionally, it seems as if both machines perform similar tasks. They both process information. They both use software—your computer uses Microsoft Word, and your brain uses context-specific bits of know-how, such as "hitting a serve," or "getting a stain out of a rug." Furthermore, both your computer and your brain are re-programmable—they aren't locked into the factory settings. Here are a few computer-inspired ideas I use to tinker with my thinking processes.

Processing Power

Your computer can only do so many things at once. It has a finite amount of processing power. The more applications you have open, the more that processing power is dispersed, and the less the computer will have available to do any given job.

---

1 Unless you're talking to them, in which case they might be able to feel your concern—and potentially be weirded out by it, depending upon the intensity.
2 And that is precisely all I know.

My brain seems to work the same way. When I find myself bogging down or getting overwhelmed, I shift my attention to programs that might be running in the background of my mind. Am I trying to do a number of things at once? Is my processing power being drained by unfounded anxieties or bits of unfinished business? If so, I need to close them before I move on to my next task.

This is by no means a perfect metaphor because it is much easier to, for example, shut down iTunes than it is to get a song out of your head. But the basic concept of limited mental power is worth keeping in mind. We seem capable of doing only so many things at once. This provides a clue for how to proceed when you feel overwhelmed. It could be that you are mentally engaging with more tasks than your brain can handle. Identifying those tasks and then approaching them one at a time may unfreeze your thought processes.

Code

Thoughts are like lines of code—which is to say, chunks of information that cause a specific effect. When you type something into a search engine and press enter, you engage many lines of code that perform a string of operations which eventually results in a list of web pages that are relevant to what you're looking for. The interesting thing about code is that in order for it to do anything, it first needs to be executed; all of the lines of code at Google just sit there until someone presses enter to engage them.

In my experience, thoughts seem to work in an analogous way. Instead of producing search results, however, thoughts tend to produce (among other things) emotions, actions, and more thoughts. The thing is, we don't realize that we have the choice to not hit enter. Thoughts arise and we immediately engage them.

Stephen Batchelor, "Buddhist teacher and author"[3] of the fascinating books *Confessions of a Buddhist Atheist* and *After Buddhism: Rethinking the Dharma for a Secular Age*, calls this tendency "reactivity." Thoughts are prompts to action that can be ignored, but more

---

3   Per his and his wife Martine's website, http://www.stephenbatchelor.org.

often than not, we react automatically and mindlessly, doing exactly what they say. In my experience, these automatic reactions are often those I most regret.

Once you begin to observe your thoughts, you will get better and better at noticing the moment they arise. That is an exciting moment. At that point, thoughts are like lines of code that have yet to be executed. With practice, you may develop the ability to choose which thoughts you execute and which you do not. The trick is to wait for the impulse to click to fade; at that point, more options will be open to you.

Viruses

A virus is a line of code that hijacks pre-existing machinery in order make copies of itself. In a sense, viruses are stupid: all they can do is copy themselves. But in another sense, viruses are smart, because they are very good at that one thing. Obviously, body cells and computers get viruses; I would make the claim that minds do, too.

Some thoughts are incredibly compelling. They make you feel like you have to spread them. I feel this way all of the time. I am just now starting to become suspicious of that feeling. It may be that I've caught a thought virus—one that serves its own purposes with little concern for my own.[4]

Structurally, I don't know if there's a fundamental difference between a pathological thought and a beneficial one. You could say that both reduce to lines of code. When I talk about a thought virus, however, I am referring to a line of code that is interested in its own replication at the expense of my well-being. Human brains are cozy places. There's a lot of glucose to live off inside of them. When I think about it that way, it's no real surprise that viruses would evolve to exploit such a food source.

That doesn't mean we have to let them. Luckily, high-quality an-

---

[4] See psychologist Susan Blackmore's *The Meme Machine* for a book-length treatment of this idea. See also marketing expert Seth Godin's *Unleashing the Ideavirus* for a more benign interpretation.

ti-viral software exists, and is relatively easy to use. It comes in the form of a question: "Why?" I try to question the ideas that want me to spread them. "Why is this compelling?" "Why do I believe this?" "Why do I feel the need to spread it?"

The more you ask yourself why thoughts seem compelling, the better you will get at recognizing whose interests they serve. Some ideas should be spread because they make people's lives better. Some ideas should be packed away because they make people's lives worse. I try to discriminate between the two. Sometimes, I succeed.

My Struggles and Suggestions

Initially, this practice hit one of my weak spots: feeling like a weirdo. Meditation can be associated with some strange beliefs. Early on in my practice, I was split between the sane, empirical results coming from groups I trusted, and the suspect assertions of groups I didn't. Could I become a serious meditator without also becoming a confused quasi-mystic? I was worried that I couldn't. I was worried that visualizations would put me on a slippery path.

Eventually, I came to realize that my resistance to these practices was underpinned by insecurity, not evidence that they wouldn't work. "OK," I told myself, "if you're as committed to honest inquiry as you say you are, your only choice is to actually give these a shot."

My first attempts were a little half-hearted, but as I continued to return to the imagery, I had to admit that it did influence my mental state, and in ways that I liked. Eventually, I was able to discern between my fear of feeling weird, and the actual results of the practice.

I now know that focusing on different types of imagery can have specific effects on my mental state. I know that, sometimes, imagining my thoughts as a lake helps me relax. Setting off sparks in my mind gets me moving. Focusing on light can be both calming and energizing. There is no reason to make any larger claims than these.

Visualization Practices work for me. If you're interested, try them for yourself.

And computers are our friends! (For now.)

Summary of the Practice

- Experiment with images of **water**. When your thoughts get out of control, imagine them sinking beneath the surface of a glassy lake. Does that help you relax?
- Experiment with images of **fire**. When your mind is cluttered with confusion or excuses, don't try to figure them out. Don't try to argue with them. Just imagine them burning away. What you need is underneath.
- Experiment with images of **light**. How would it feel to imagine yourself glowing from the inside? Would you relate to other people differently if they were glowing from the inside? Imagine they are, and see what happens.
- Allow yourself to think of your thoughts and beliefs as **lines of code**. Can you develop the ability to notice them when they appear? Do you have to let them trigger behavior, or can you refuse to hit enter?

FINAL THOUGHTS:
Walking the Maze

HERE WE ARE AT THE END of a book that I wasn't even sure I should write.

We've talked about four different meditative practices: practices to train focus, practices to look more closely at the stuff of experience, practices to train positive emotions, and visualizations to disrupt unhelpful moods.

In **Focus Practices**, you select an object of focus—interior **body sensations** or the **sensations of your breath** being common ones—and train your attention to remain with that object. You will continually be distracted. The practice involves noticing that distraction and returning again and again to your chosen object. In time, you'll find that you have more choice as to what you focus on.

In **Insight Practices**, you use your improving concentration to mentally probe four types of objects: **bodily sensations**, **feeling-tones**, **thoughts**, and the **relationships** between things in the world. You use three questions ("Is this permanent?" "Is this a source of happiness?"

"Is this me?") to look more closely at them. In the case of relationships, you can ask, "What does this depend on?"

The **Positive Emotion Practices** use specific phrases to train helpful states of mind. You practice generating feelings of **goodwill**, **compassion**, and **positive empathy** towards different people. You also cultivate **poise** in response to challenging situations. As I see it, positivity is about identifying and solving problems, and it's hard to do so when you yourself are down in the dumps.

Finally, the **Visualization Practices** use specific imagery to help you shift your moment-to-moment state of mind when necessary. We talked about using images of **water** to calm your thoughts when they're out of control, images of **fire** to cut through your thoughts when they're limiting, and images of **light** as a general tool for clearing you head. We also talked about some concepts from **computing** and ways you might use them to evaluate the quality of your own thinking.

I personally started meditating because it sounded like a cool thing to do. Monks do it, and they seem cool. Brain scientists do it (or at least study it), and they seem cool. Phil Jackson had players on the Lakers basketball team do it, and they won a lot of championships. With so many seemingly respectable sources speaking out about the benefits of a given practice, it was hard to believe that they were all making it up. I figured I had to see what the fuss was about.

The truth is that my own experience with meditation has been rocky. I started practicing without knowing what I was doing. That isn't necessarily a problem—in fact, that's probably the only way you can start anything. But meditation isn't quite like learning a new sport or picking up an instrument. There is potentially a lot more at stake: your sanity.

Many different types of people meditate, and they have just as many different beliefs regarding what the practice implies. These beliefs range from suggestions for effective ways to live a more careful life to speculations about the metaphysical structure of the universe. It's relatively easy to get into meditation for the brain science and then to be sucked unknowingly into the metaphysics. It's worth being aware of this possibility before starting a practice. I've learned to guard my beliefs somewhat carefully.

As I see it, the meditative practices we have discussed are first and foremost tools for familiarizing oneself with the actual quality of your daily life. They are most effectively used as ways of gathering information about your habits for the purpose of evaluating the degree to which they are helpful. In practice, this requires that you perform a close examination of the relationship between your habits, the beliefs that inform those habits, and the evidence that in turn informs those beliefs. Treated this way, meditation can be seen as an application of basic scientific principles (skepticism, empiricism, hypothesis-formation, intellectual honesty) to one's internal life, with the aim of becoming aware of previously automatic and destructive behavior patterns so that they can be (slowly) corrected.

I do my best to meditate at least once a day, though ideally I aim for two sessions. I meditate in the morning for at least a half-hour (sometimes I make time for a forty-five-minute session), and try to add a second, shorter session (twenty minutes) at another point during the day. I do miss sessions, but I know that one missed session leads quite easily to more missed sessions, so I try to be careful. I dedicate most sessions to Focus Practices. During the day, I do my best to be aware of the thoughts and emotions that prompt my behavior. I try with varying degrees of success to evaluate the usefulness of that behavior before engaging in it. While I'm far from perfect, I find that my actions are more conscious and intentional than they used to be, which is ultimately all I am aiming for.

I hope I've convinced you to give meditation a shot. Along the way you may fall into many of the same traps that I did (and continue to). You may confuse repression for relaxation. You may confuse apathy for poise. You may confuse self-righteousness for concern. Or you may not. The only one who can really know your inner life is you. That knowledge has to be gained, however, through careful—and sometimes painful—work.

In my experience, the contemplative journey is one worth taking. As long as you are careful to stick to the facts of your actual experience, you will probably find that you are less distracted, less irritated, less confused, and less angry more and more of the time. This means that you will have much more attention and energy to devote to things that you care about, rather than being bogged down by things that you don't.

At least, that's the hypothesis. Test it for yourself.

APPENDIX:
Further Reading

I'VE READ WAY TOO MANY MEDITATION BOOKS. You might be careful about getting lost in the literature, but in case you're interested here are a few that I've found useful. They are ordered from the scientifically-minded to the more speculative. There is some weird stuff out there. Watch out for it.

Safe for Skeptics

Waking Up: A Guide to Spirituality Without Religion—Sam Harris

Sam Harris is best known for being an outspoken critic of organized religion. What many may not know is that Sam is also an experienced meditator. In this particular book, he shares his experiences as such, and makes a case for ways to integrate contemplative practices into a non-religious, scientific mindset. While I do worry about his rhetorical decisions (his language use can be uncompromising in ways that seem to me to be unproductive), I consider Sam to be a mentor, and feel greatly indebted to his work. This book helped me ground a meditative practice in intellectual values that I identify with.

10% Happier: How I Tamed the Voice in My Head, Reduced Stress Without Losing My Edge, and Found Self-Help That Actually Works—A True Story—Dan Harris

Dan Harris (no relation to Sam) is a television anchor with NBC news. In this book, he shares how he first got into meditation after a drug-induced panic attack on national TV. He talks about working through his resistance towards starting and maintaining a meditative practice as someone employed in a competitive industry. This book is honest and hilarious and (at times) vulgar, and helped me to lighten up when I was taking meditation too seriously.

The Emotional Life of Your Brain—Richard Davidson

In this book, Richard Davidson presents the results of his research on the brains of advanced meditators. This is the book that first got me seriously interested in meditation. It presents rigorous scientific findings in a way that is accessible to those without a background in neuroscience, and provides empirical evidence in which to ground theory on why meditation works.

Focus: The Hidden Driver of Excellence—Daniel Goleman

In this book, psychologist and journalist Daniel Goleman—who coined the term *emotional intelligence*—summarizes research on attention. He uses case studies to show both how it is useful and how to improve it. This book got me interested in Focus Practices.

The Willpower Instinct—Kelly McGonigal

Kelly McGonigal is a health psychologist and highly-regarded instructor in Stanford's Continuing Studies program. This book provides an incredible wealth of information on the science of human behavior change—what's even more valuable, however, is the wealth of practical and immediately actionable insight it derives from that research.

As I understand it, this book emerged out of a course McGonigal has taught in said program called "The Science of Willpower." The course has been open to the general public and appears to be highly regarded—if the book is any indication of its quality, I wouldn't be at all surprised. It is very rigorous in its treatment of the research while remaining both accessible to a non-academic audience and eminently applicable to everyday life. In my opinion, this book is probably far more useful than the one you have just read.

My Number One Recommendation for Practice Instructions

The Mind Illuminated: A Complete Meditation Guide Integrating Buddhist Wisdom and Brain Science—Culadasa (John Yates, Ph.D), Matthew Immergut, and Jeremy Graves

It's hard for me to overstate my love for this book. It is both the most comprehensive and most comprehensible meditation manual I have encountered—one that really does seem to integrate Buddhist traditional practice instructions with brain science. As of this writing, I practice according to the instructions in this book. They are primarily tailored to Focus Practices. It's worth noting that I was already quite familiar with meditative traditions and basic cognitive science when I read this book. It may be a little challenging for those who are new to those fields, but generally it is the most accessible meditation text I have encountered. It's also worth noting that the book is organized according to stages of competency, and some of the later stages are categorized by levels of focus that strain my credulity. This isn't to say that I believe they are fanciful, merely that I personally relate more to the beginning levels, which match my experience quite closely.

More Detail On the Practices—Largely Buddhist

Minding Closely: The Four Applications of Mindfulness
—Alan B. Wallace

Alan B. Wallace is another Westerner who was trained in the Tibetan Buddhist tradition. In this book, he explicates the four Insight Practices. I find Wallace to be a sharp thinker in many ways, though it's worth noting that he speaks from within a particular belief system that I do not hold. I choose to reject some of the metaphysical claims he sometimes seems to make, but his firsthand experience with Insight Practices is very useful.

Lovingkindness: The Revolutionary Art of Happiness
—Sharon Salzburg

This book informs my understanding of the Positive Emotion Practices. Salzburg gives a very personal account of her experience with them, and also provides detailed and very accessible instructions of how to engage with them. As with Wallace, she also speaks from within a Buddhist worldview, but she does do a good job of drawing clear distinctions between Buddhist beliefs and more universal practice instructions. Her personal story is also honest and relatable, and provides compelling reasons to try the practices.

Why Meditate? Working with Thoughts and Emotions
—Matthieu Ricard

Matthieu Ricard is a Frenchman who was originally trained as a biologist before eventually becoming a monk in a Tibetan tradition. This book is short and accessible. It also speaks from Buddhist traditions, and tends towards poetic imagery (which contrasts a bit with the more nuts and bolts descriptions provided by Culadasa in the above recommendation). I found it to be a good entry point to meditative practices. It's also where I got some of the imagery in the visualization section. Interestingly, Ricard was one of the meditators whose brain Richard Davidson studied.

The War of Art—Stephen Pressfield

This book isn't about meditation per se, but I think it should be required reading for anyone attempting to develop a new habit. Pressfield, the author of a number of books including *The Legend of Bagger*

Vance, writes eloquently about the challenges involved in developing any kind of creative practice, be it writing, painting, making an album, starting a business, or anything else that requires you to recommit to a daily struggle. I think that it speaks beautifully to the type of attitudes that benefit a would-be meditator.

Ego is the Enemy—Ryan Holiday

It's relatively easy to say that one's true enemy lies within. It's considerably more difficult to do the work to tame it. The first step, perhaps, is familiarizing oneself with how that enemy works. What exactly does it feel like to be under the spell of the ego? In this book, Ryan Holiday—a former ad executive at American Apparel and the author of *Trust Me, I'm Lying: Confessions of a Media Manipulator*—paints a compelling picture of both the kind of damage your ego can do and a few early warning signs you can use to determine whether or not you need to make a course correction. If meditation has taught me anything, it's that one correction is not enough. Keeping to the straight and narrow seems to require constant attention. This book, I think, has at least given me an idea of how to find the right line. It might do the same for you, too.

Practice Tools (Not Books)

Headspace—Phone App

After mentioning it earlier in this book, I've spent some time experimenting with Headspace. I now think it is a great app. It could really help someone to start a practice. It has a number of guided meditations (some are free, but most require a paid subscription), and a few high-quality animations to explain basic concepts. It also utilizes tips from behavioral psychology to help you establish a meditation habit. I would definitely recommend downloading the app and trying the free meditations if you're new. It might be worth a shot even if you're not new! I've always been a little bit resistant to guided meditations (because I have a tendency to want to do things the hard way, which isn't necessarily something to be proud of), but I like these ones.

eSangha—A Community of Practice

Tucker Peck, meditation teacher and clinical psychologist, runs a weekly meditation group through Google Chat that he calls eSangha. His website is meditatewithtucker.com, which you can visit for more information. I am not a regular attendee of eSangha because I tend to be a bit of a loner, but I have enjoyed myself every time I have attended. Tucker is very knowledgeable, both in terms of meditation experience and brain science (he has a Ph.D. in clinical psychology) and is very good at connecting with a wide range of people. Furthermore, the philosophy of the group matches (and has influenced) mine: "This class has no dogma, and anytime I reference the Buddha, it's simply because he said something that I've found to be true, and he said it better than I could. The methods and teachings you'll learn about should all be considered hypotheses for you to test, not absolute truth."[1] Not everyone is interested in joining a meditation group, but if you are, I would recommend looking into Tucker's to see if it is right for you.

Weird but Interesting—Care Required (Back to Books)

The Book On the Taboo Against Knowing Who You Are
—Alan Watts

When I think of white guys who are into Eastern philosophy, Alan Watts is the first one who comes to mind. He is a prolific writer who published a large number of books (he passed away in 1973), many of which I thoroughly enjoyed reading. This particular book made me rethink the way I related to my thoughts. Watts is also all over the place at times, but I've always found him a pleasure to read.

---

[1] Per Tucker's website: http://meditatewithtucker.com/online-meditation-class/.

If You Find Yourself Drifting into Pseudoscience/Lunacy

Faith vs. Fact: Why Science and Religion Are Incompatible
—Jerry Coyne

Jerry Coyne is a biologist whose recent work has been to make the theory of evolution accessible to a popular audience. In this particular book, he provides a framework for clear and critical thinking. His primary aim is to provide methods for evaluating truth claims. You don't necessarily have to accept the conclusion that forms the subtitle of the book, but I personally found his methods to be very valuable as I tried to navigate the meditation literature. Some meditators make truth claims that are hard to assess, and this book gave me the tools to separate evidence from wishful thinking.

After Buddhism: Rethinking the Dharma for a Secular Age
—Stephen Batchelor

Stephen Batchelor is a Scottish man who became a monk in a Tibetan tradition in the 1970's. Unlike Alan Wallace and Matthieu Ricard, he eventually left the order (at least, that's my understanding; his website says he "disrobed in February 1985"[2]). Many Westerners feel that Eastern religions (and particularly Buddhism) are free of disagreement and discord. I was one such person. Batchelor challenges those beliefs. His scholarship deals with the complicated history of Buddhist communities in an attempt to separate the teachings of a man named Siddhartha Gautama from possible later monastic additions. This is a somewhat scholarly work that might not be interesting for everyone, but it helped me to recognize when I was idealizing Buddhism with less than helpful results.

---

2   http://www.stephenbatchelor.org/index.php/en/stephen/biography

Colophon

This book was designed by Dana Johnson using Adobe InDesign CC.

The text is set in Adelle and Adelle Sans, designed by Veronika Burian and José Scaglione, and Proxima Nova, designed by Mark Simonson.

CHAD FRISK started meditating in 2011 after encountering the subject in connection to neuroscience. From that point on, he has worked to integrate a meditative practice into a scientific worldview. The work continues, but he currently thinks of meditation as a set of tools for engaging in careful, reasoned, and informed inquiry of first-person experience. He thinks it is important that any individual interested in using these tools assume responsibility for making sense of them on his or her own, but he is happy to share his process for potential reference.

www.ingramcontent.com/pod-product-compliance
Lightning Source LLC
Chambersburg PA
CBHW060813050426
42449CB00008B/1651